Restraint of Trade

Fourmat Publishing

Restraint of Trade

by Jacqueline Wilkinson, BA, Solicitor
Lecturer in Law

London
Fourmat Publishing
1991

ISBN 1 85190 140 X

First published 1991

© 1991 Jacqueline Wilkinson
Published by Fourmat Publishing, 133 Upper Street,
London N1 1QP

Printed in Great Britain by
Billing and Sons Limited, Worcester

For Connie and Rowland Wilkinson

Preface

It is perhaps strange justification for a book that many lawyers think its subject-matter irrelevant or not worth taking into consideration in modern times. They are, however, wrong, as this book is written to show. I was always surprised in practice by the cavalier attitude taken by many practitioners to covenants in restraint of trade. When I began researching this book, my surprise turned to concern as I began to encounter cases where legal advisers had sweepingly advised that this or that covenant was too wide to be enforceable, only to have it upheld against their clients. Similarly, there have been cases where professionally drafted covenants have failed to protect the client. These are not borderline cases but cases where a little attention to the rules of the doctrine would have highlighted the error before it could cause any harm.

This book is aimed primarily at the practitioner, and especially the practitioner who may not have considered the restraint clauses in a contract to be worthy of special consideration or to be governed by any specifically identifiable rules. There are rules and guidelines — many of them — which emerge from a thorough reading of the case law and in this book I aim to identify those rules and guidelines in such a way that they enable a restraint to be evaluated or drafted with a reasonable degree of certainty (although of course with a doctrine based on reasonableness one can never be absolutely certain whether a covenant is likely to be upheld or not). I have included chapters on advising the client from both angles, and on the principles of drafting a restrictive covenant. I am well aware that I am leaving myself open to a charge of "teaching my grandmother to suck eggs" here, and I am sure that many of my readers will have precedents which they prefer to the examples I have given. Nevertheless, even they may not be aware of some of the more recent decisions which have a knock-on effect on how a covenant should be drafted, and it is quite clear from the cases that there are enough practitioners out there who do not know how to draft a suitable covenant, to make it worthwhile including them. The articled clerk and novice solicitor will, I hope, find both chapters very useful.

As a teacher, I could not forget the law student in writing this work and I have chosen to concentrate particular attention on a small number of more recent cases concerning the doctrine to try and establish whether it is possible to detect a shift in the way the court is considering these covenants in modern times. It is my view that there is the urge to shift ground in response to what the courts see as the modern public interest, but that the shift is still in the process of being worked out through the cases. Students and other teachers may disagree with me but the object is to bring the subject back within the forum of discussion.

Finally, the doctrine can no longer be considered without some attention being paid to its legislative companions — restrictive practices, resale price maintenance and EEC competition law — and its equitable partners, the duties of confidentiality and fidelity. It would be useless in a modest work of this nature to try and cover these topics in any great detail but I have tried to include the basic principles and some examples with a view to demonstrating how these three areas interconnect and to warning practitioners that there is more than the restraint doctrine alone to be taken into consideration when advising upon or drafting a restraint clause.

In conclusion, I wish to thank the many people who have encouraged and supported me in my first full-length work, especially David and Rosalind Maxwell-Harrison and colleagues at Leicester Polytechnic, and Richard Clark who taught me my first principles of drafting.

Thanks also go to The Incorporated Council of Law Reporting for England and Wales, Butterworths, Sweet & Maxwell and IRS for their permission to use the quotations included in the work.

Jacqueline Wilkinson
July 1991

Contents

Table of cases

Introduction

The restraint of trade doctrine has been with us in one form or another for at least four hundred years. Its heyday was the period between 1890 and 1920 when it underwent a process of formation and development which left us with broadly the principles which we have today. The original purpose of the doctrine was to strike at anti-competitive practices at a time when there was no other means of doing so. As such it was not perhaps the best tool for the job, but it was the best the courts could devise within the context of the developing law of contract.

Nearly a hundred years on, the doctrine is still with us, not, as some may think, a limping Victorian ghost whose task has been taken over by something better suited for the purpose, but as a vigorous weapon which may be used by the court to strike at injustice and unconscionable bargains. This is not perhaps quite the purpose for which it was originally intended but one which, in the absence of another instrument, can be seen to be effective.

Roughly half way through the century, the legislature realised the deficiencies in the doctrine when it came to controlling monopolies and many other undesirable anti-competitive practices, and embarked on the legislative reforms we now know as the restrictive practices and resale price maintenance legislation. In considering restraint of trade, these forms of statutory regulation cannot be ignored as they overlap and operate hand-in-hand with the restraint doctrine. Although they can strike at many practices which were for various reasons beyond the scope of the doctrine, there are areas of restraint of trade which they do not cover, agreements which are not included within their ambit, and here the restraint doctrine will take over and fill any gaps left by the legislation. The whole area of restrictions in employment contracts, for example, as well as many other agreements, is exempt from the scope of the legislation. It would therefore be wrong to try to write a book on restraint of trade without including something about restrictive trade practices and resale price maintenance. Nevertheless, a full review of the legislation is way beyond the scope of this work and only a summary, together with some points of interest on how the legislation works in with the doctrine, is given, and the reader is directed to specialist works on the subject.

In recent years, EEC competition law has come to the fore. Articles 85 and 86 of the Treaty of Rome have far-reaching effects on agreements, particularly in relation to matters which are within the scope of the doctrine, as well as many which are outside it. However, the Articles do not apply to every agreement. In fact, restrictions which do not affect inter-member trade will not fall within the scope of either Article 85 or Article 86. Nevertheless, as explained in Chapter 7, this condition is nowhere near as onerous as might be thought at first glance, and transactions which one might not expect to be caught by EEC law are in fact caught. Again, EEC competition law is a specialist subject with an enormous body of case law, so that it has not been possible to include more than a simple summary and some examples. These are designed to alert the unwary to restrictions which may be caught by the provisions of the Treaty, although it may not be immediately apparent that one or other of the Articles applies. Where an agreement is caught by either Article 85 or Article 86, therefore, there may be an overlap with our national law on restrictive trade practices and resale price maintenance and also the restraint doctrine, so a covenantee may find himself in double jeopardy and, if he is not to be trapped in this way, the rules applicable in each field must be considered in conjunction.

The restraint of trade doctrine, together with its legislative brethren, therefore provides a formidable enemy to the anti-competitive restriction in an agreement, but there is yet another rapidly developing area by which implied equitable duties are used to control the other contractual party rather than express contractual duties. These include duties of good faith and confidentiality and, since there is a growing interchange between their rules and the restraint of trade doctrine, they cannot be ignored in any examination of the modern application of the doctrine.

The following chapters then attempt to assist the lawyer to find his way through the maze of legislative, equitable and common law rules so that he can evaluate or draft a restraint of trade clause with reasonable confidence that it is likely to be upheld by the law. Restraint of trade is a doctrine founded on public policy and one therefore expects the courts to shift ground continually in response to what they believe to be the current pressures imposed on them by the public interest. Many of the most recent cases are therefore examined in detail to try to establish just where the court considers current public interest to lie. Are the courts still fettered by the Victorian rules or have they struck out on a new path? Does their reasoning reflect the public interest as it exists today? These points are undoubtedly of interest to the academic lawyer for it is in areas such as this where the courts have more or less free rein on policy that one can detect changes in the direction of the court's thinking which may extend to other areas. For the practising lawyer, who is in the front line of drafting an agreement which will "stick" not only now but at some unknown time in the future, it is always useful to have some idea of the court's current thinking and the direction in which it may be likely to go in the foreseeable future.

While not neglecting the academic points, a great deal of emphasis is laid on advising the client, and drafting restraints which are likely to be upheld should they come to be considered in court. Any idea that the restraint doctrine and its equitable companions are subject to the whim of the courts is wrong. There are clear patterns and guidelines and this work attempts to identify them and put them to practical use. It is the author's intention and hope that both the academic and the practising lawyer will find something in the following chapters which will be of interest and help to them.

Chapter 1

The scope of the restraint of trade doctrine

The original doctrine in restraint of trade was created over four hundred years ago to curb the abuse of a monopolistic position held in the market by traders who had been fortunate enough to win royal favour. During the last two decades of the nineteenth century and the first two decades of the twentieth century, the doctrine underwent a considerable period of expansion and development, in which many of the fundamental principles of the doctrine were laid down. During this period, the public policy which the courts were anxious to enforce was that every man should have the right to work and to offer his services freely in the market place. The courts also developed the fundamental principle that, while the vendor and purchaser of a business being on equal footing were entitled to include in their agreement almost any restriction they wished and have it upheld by the court, an employer, being in a far stronger bargaining position than his employee, ought to be restrained from using that position to impose restraints which would fetter the employee too restrictively. Restraints which were thought to be excessive were struck down in the public interest. In this period of development, most agreements which came before the courts for consideration could be fitted within the model of either a vendor-purchaser agreement or an employer-employee agreement. Those which could not were not usually subjected to the doctrine.

There then followed a period of some forty years during which the courts applied the rules laid down by their Victorian and Edwardian predecessors, and the doctrine was regarded as having very sharp teeth which would bite with particular force on

1

employer-employee restrictions, so that it seemed for a time that it was scarcely possible for an employer to restrain his employee from working for a competitor after termination of his employment unless the employee possessed trade secrets or had a strong influence over his customers.

The next period of development, which has continued to the present day, has required the courts to consider an increasing number of "hybrid" agreements which cannot be fitted easily into either the vendor-purchaser category or the employer-employee mould. Although the courts still insist on these categories as providing a means of deciding whether clauses in restraint of trade should be upheld, they have at the same time had to develop new tests for determining whether or not the restraint is too great a fetter on the convenantor's liberty.

A further, more recent, development which is also continuing, has been brought about by legislative provisions aimed at areas where the doctrine is less effective, and by the EEC competition policy which this country, like all member-states of the Community, is bound to implement. The doctrine has had to move its position once again to accommodate these new and, in some cases, better methods of dealing with abuse of position by the imposition of restrictions on the right to trade. We now see the doctrine taking over new ground and, in areas not covered by the legislation, striking at injustice and the unfair or unethical treatment of one party by another.

Far from being a dead, useless or irrelevant doctrine, restraint of trade continues to develop in response to attempts to avoid its operation. It may be that as the courts become more used to applying the unfamiliar principles of EEC law, these will be imported into the restraint of trade doctrine to strengthen and make consistent those areas which EEC law does not reach. The doctrine will not disappear and it is worth taking a good look at it as it stands today.

It is often thought that, because it is a public policy doctrine, no clear rules can be stated for its operation. This is certainly not true. The case law may be confused by the courts' tendency to shift ground from time to time, but there are clear rules and guidelines which make it possible to draft an effective restrictive covenant or to evaluate the likely effectiveness or otherwise of a covenant upon which one is asked to give advice. It is not true, as some believe and several have found to their cost, that all covenants in restraint of trade are void. Nor is it true that some types of covenant will automatically be upheld. It is a question of examining the circumstances of each case.

This chapter considers the broad scope of the doctrine and summarises the basic rules for its operation. In the following chapters, the most common categories of agreement in which restraints are to be found are considered in detail to discover the particular points which the courts take into consideration and to establish guidelines for assessing the validity of the restraint.

1. When does the doctrine apply?

The restraint of trade doctrine itself can be stated simply in a single sentence: *a contract in restraint of trade is void unless it can be shown to be reasonable.* However, the courts have consistently taken a cautious approach to defining the phrase "contract in restraint of trade", and to identify a contract which is likely to fall foul of the doctrine is not always an easy task. Even the phrase itself has been used in two senses by courts, sometimes to mean a contract which contains a restraint clause, and sometimes to mean the restraint clause itself. (In this book, where the phrase is used it will have the latter meaning.)

Although usually considered as a contractual doctrine, actions for restraint of trade have even been used to strike at restrictive practices outside the ambit of contract. In *Nagle v Feilden* (1966) for example, a female trainer of racehorses was consistently refused a licence by the Jockey Club. The court held that the practice of excluding women could be deemed in restraint of trade. However, such instances are fairly rare and other actions have developed to deal with them. We will mainly be concerned, therefore, with contractual restraints, and in particular the most common forms of contractual restraint to be met in practice.

The doctrine is usually invoked against post-termination or post-completion restraints, ie those which are expressed to continue after completion of the contract or after the relationship between the parties has been determined. There appears to be some doubt as to whether the doctrine can be invoked to strike down restraints during the currency of an agreement. There are dicta of Lord Pearce (*Esso Petroleum Co Ltd* v *Harper's Garage (Stourport) Ltd* [1968] AC 269 at page 326) which have been taken to suggest otherwise, but the ratio of the case clearly shows that it can, although only in the case of a party so unilaterally fettered

3

that the contract no longer regulates or promotes trade but takes on the predominating character of restriction.

The doctrine began its life in the Elizabethan courts which were primarily concerned with the increase in monopolies and which held all restraints of trade to be void. The practical effects of this policy were soon seen to have devastating consequences for trade and the courts quickly saw the need to relax their rigid approach. Initially the doctrine was applied to contracts of employment, contracts for the sale of a business and contracts to create a monopoly. It was not until the "solus agreement" cases of the 1960s that the question of whether the doctrine applied to other types of contract came to be fully discussed in the higher courts — decisions in the interim were often confused as to whether a restraint was allowable because the doctrine did not apply or because it was unreasonable. In *Petrofina (Great Britain) Ltd v Martin* (1966), Diplock LJ proposed a definition which has received wide approval:

> "a contract in restraint of trade is one in which a party (the covenantor) agrees with any other party (the covenantee) to restrict his liberty in the future to carry on trade with other parties not parties to the contract in such a manner as he chooses."

This definition is not without flaw, as Lord Wilberforce noted in *Esso Petroleum Co Ltd v Harper's Garage (Stourport) Ltd*. Although attacking the generality of this and other previous formulations, his lordship nevertheless declined to substitute a definition of his own, on the ground that the doctrine rests on public policy which would, in his opinion, have been a mistake to crystallise into neat propositions.

(a) Are any contracts exempt from the doctrine?

In the absence of a clear definition, lawyers have frequently sought to argue that there are classes of contract which by their very nature are free from scrutiny under the doctrine. This argument was put forward in *Esso v Harper's Garage* where it was shown to be an unsafe proposition. The respondents were owners of two garages who entered into separate agreements, called "solus agreements", for different periods under which they covenanted to buy petrol exclusively from the appellants, to re-sell only at certain prices, to keep the garage open at all hours and, on selling or otherwise disposing of the garages, to procure that the new occupant entered into similar agreement, with the appellants. One of the garages was mortgaged to the appellants and the mortgage contained similar covenants. The respondents claimed that these agreements were void for restraint of trade.

It was argued on behalf of the appellants that, amongst other things, the restrictions in the agreements were restrictive covenants which imposed a burden on the land analogous to those often contained in conveyances, leases or mortgages, which were subject to the rules in *Tulk* v *Moxhay* (1848) and could not therefore be subjected to the doctrine. The House of Lords, while reluctantly accepting that restrictive covenants could not be tested for reasonableness, found no difficulty in deciding that covenants, including those in question, which were not purely "ordinary negative covenants" could be tested with reference to the doctrine.

In *Petrofina* v *Martin*, where the facts were similar to those in *Esso* save for the fact that the covenants were "in gross" rather than being attached to the land, and the respondent was not the original covenantor, the Court of Appeal had earlier arrived at a similar conclusion, albeit for different reasons.

It was made particularly clear in the *Esso* case that the nature of the contract of itself, even if it were a mortgage, lease or conveyance, could not prevent the court from applying the doctrine. In reaching this conclusion, the court was faced with a considerable body of authority in which previous courts had upheld similar covenants tying public houses to sell the products of particular brewery companies. Some commentators had deemed such "tied houses" agreements to be exempt from the doctrine. Although it is clear that there may be a form of exemption where the agreement is in the customary form, the draftsman is advised to tread warily. Lord Wilberforce emphasised that in order for the court to look favourably upon such an agreement it must be confined strictly within the accepted boundaries:

> " . . . they have become part of the accepted machinery of a type of transaction which is generally found acceptable and necessary, so that instead of being regarded as restrictive they are accepted as part of the structure of a trading society."

If there is anything unusual about the agreement or if there is a greater restriction than usual or the agreement has been used as a device to evade the doctrine, the courts will subject the agreement, notwithstanding that it is in the standard form, to the application of the doctrine.

It is still not absolutely clear whether agreements which do not deviate from the standard are in fact totally exempt from the doctrine or whether they are to be deemed automatically reasonable. The words of Lord Wilberforce quoted above would seem to suggest the latter view is correct. Negotiation between parties on an equal footing, together with customary usage over a long period of time, will, it seems, have the effect of "sanctifying" a restriction so that it cannot be said to be unreasonable (see *Schroeder Music Publishing Co Ltd v Macaulay* (1974) below), but the courts are not precluded from examining a restriction which in any way deviates from the norm, so the agreements are in reality not exempt at all. This may also be seen as part of the reasoning which distinguishes the older trade association cases of *McEllistrim v Ballymacelligott Co-operative Agricultural and Dairy Society* (1919) and *English Hop Growers Ltd v Dering* (1928) (see Chapter 5).

There is a further category of contractual restrictions with which the courts are unlikely to interfere. These are where there is an alternative or superior method of scrutiny which has been developed either in another branch of the law or by the legislature. An obvious example is the restrictive trade practices legislation which relieved the courts of having to decide whether such practices fell within the restraint of trade doctrine (although it does not mean that agreements subject to the legislation are exempt from the doctrine − a restrictive practice which escapes the legislative framework may still be caught by the doctrine).

(b) Let the draftsman beware!

The following conclusions can be drawn from the above:

- post-termination restraints in contracts of employment and post-completion restraints in a contract for the sale of the goodwill of a business can and will be subjected to the reasonableness test;

- while the courts are prevented from subjecting to the reasonableness test pure negative restrictive covenants which burden the land only, they are not precluded from examining restrictions of other kinds in leases, conveyances, mortgages and the like which are, or might be considered to be, in restraint of trade;

- there is no contract in restraint of trade which the court cannot subject to the test of reasonableness, but it will usually decline to invoke the doctrine when there is a standard form of contract sanctified by negotiation by parties on an equal footing and long usage; it will allow the doctrine to be used only where an agreement contains unusual provisions;

- there are some contracts in restraint of trade which do not need to be subjected to the doctrine because other, more suitable, provisions exist for testing them, and the tests are likely to be more stringent;

- the doctrine will not normally apply to restrictions during the continuance of the contract, even if they exclude all dealings with others, provided that they are incidental and normal to the positive commercial arrangements at which the contract aims; it will apply, however, if the restrictions so unilaterally fetter one of the parties that the agreement sterilises his services and stifles, rather than promotes, trade.

The *Esso* and *Petrofina* cases are discussed in more detail in Chapter 5.

2. Public policy

The doctrine is based on public policy, which is often confused with public interest, although these are not always the same thing.

Public policy is an ever-changing concept (Lord Pearce compared it to an unruly horse) and where the doctrine in question is over three hundred years old, shifts in policy may explain sometimes irreconcilable decisions. However, in trying to apply what they consider to be current public policy, the courts sometimes confuse the issues and arrive at decisions which may not always appear justifiable on a strict application of rules to the facts – as will be shown later.

The earliest reported consideration of public policy is to be found in Parker CJ's judgment in *Mitchel* v *Reynolds* (1711). He identified three public policy reasons why contracts in restraint of trade might be deemed bad:

(a) the loss to the public of a man carrying on his trade;

(b) the detrimental effect on competition;

(c) where the restraint is voluntary (ie without consideration) no benefit accrues to the covenantor and enforcement is contrary to usual contractual principles.

In *Nordenfelt* v *Maxim Nordenfelt Guns and Ammunition Co* [1894] AC 535, a case concerning a worldwide restraint on the seller of a business from competing with the buyer, Lord Macnaghten formulated public policy in terms of public interest:

> "The public have an interest in every person's carrying on his trade freely; so has the individual. All interference with individual liberty of action in trading, and all restraints of trade of themselves, if there is nothing more, are contrary to public policy, and therefore void" (page 565).

It is worth noting that, in common with his contemporaries, Lord Macnaghten took it for granted that freedom of trade was in the public interest and found it unnecessary to support his opinion. In the climate of Victorian expansionism, no explanation was necessary. Today, however, we have perhaps become more used to restrictions and it is recognised that safeguards are often necessary. Accordingly the public may be more inclined to accept trade restrictions for its own benefit.

In *Herbert Morris Ltd* v *Saxelby* (1916), in which employers sought to restrain an ex-employee by a term in his contract of employment from being engaged in a competing business after termination of his employment, Lord Atkinson considered the two competing requirements of public policy, which were:

(i) that everyone is free to work and no one can contract in such a way as to deprive himself or the State of his labour, talents or skills; and

(ii) that where a man has something to sell and can only sell it profitably by inserting provisions in the contract restricting his freedom to compete, public policy requires that he be allowed to do so.

This has sometimes been described as the right to work versus the right to bargain.

This dichotomy which has bedevilled the doctrine since the nineteenth century set in opposition two fundamental Victorian ideals: that a person of full age and legal competence should be free to make any contract he chooses, so long as it is not illegal, and that everyone is free to trade, compete and offer his skills in the market place. In an age of *laissez-faire* such as that in which the doctrine was first shaped, each of these principles was of equal importance. Students of the operation of the doctrine in modern times need to consider to what extent this is still the case. Much of the case law on the subject is concerned with the courts' attempts to reconcile these two competing freedoms, and at various times freedom of contract has triumphed over freedom of trade, and vice versa.

When considering older precedents which the courts use to justify their modern decisions, therefore, it is worth noting the economic theory prevailing at the time the older decision was made. The "public policy" pendulum has so often swung back and forth that it is perhaps true to say that any judge who takes a pragmatic view of the case can find authority for his viewpoint.

The reasonableness requirement has in later times been used to balance the two principles. Before taking a look at this requirement, however, it is interesting to note a more recent approach to the question of public policy taken by Lord Diplock in *Schroeder Music Publishing Co Ltd* v *Macaulay* (1974):

> " ... the public policy which the court is implementing is not some nineteenth century economic theory about the benefit to the general public of freedom of trade, but the protection of those whose bargaining power is weak against being forced by those whose bargaining power is stronger to enter bargains which are unconscionable."

In other words, a more modern use of the restraint doctrine has been to strike at unconscionable bargains. This use of a common law doctrine for an equitable purpose is interesting and, as will be seen later, is not the only example of how equity may colour the court's thinking on the doctrine.

3. Reasonableness

The second limb of the doctrine states that a contract in restraint of trade will not be void so long as it is reasonable.

During the eighteenth and nineteenth centuries, two main principles developed: first, that all general restraints were void — "general" meaning not limited in time or space; second, that if a partial (limited) restraint was supported by sufficient consideration it should usually be upheld. The limitation and the consideration were enough to make it reasonable. Notwithstanding later developments, elements of this view can still be seen in modern cases.

In the *Nordenfelt* case, the House of Lords exploded the first and weakened the second of these principles. It held that a general restraint could be valid provided that it was reasonable in the circumstances considered at the time the contract was made. Regardless of whether the restraint was general or partial, consideration was merely one of the factors to be taken into account when determining the reasonableness or otherwise of the restraint.

The court will look at what the covenantor is getting in return for his covenant, monetary consideration being an obvious example, of course, but in line with principles of consideration generally, it will not look at the sufficiency of the consideration.

After stating the general public policy rule as quoted above, Lord Macnaghten went on to explain in an oft-quoted passage that there were exceptions to the general rule that restraints of trade were contrary to public policy. The use of a restraint, he considered, might be justified by the special circumstances of the case which would show that the restraint was both reasonable in the interest of the parties and reasonable in the public interest. In other words it must be no more restrictive than necessary to protect the covenantee while not being in any way injurious to the public. If a restraint could pass that test, then it would be upheld.

This passage of Lord Macnaghten's judgment is worth reading since the courts have used it as a cornerstone of their judgments ever since, albeit with varying interpretations.

It is quite clear that Lord Macnaghten believed there were two limbs to the reasonableness requirement: reasonableness in the parties' interests and reasonableness in the public interest. It has since been established that the onus of proving the former was on the party seeking to validate the covenant and the latter on the other party (*Attorney-General of Commonwealth of Australia* v *Adelaide Steamship Co Ltd* (1913), although for practical purposes this probably no longer matters (see, for example, Lord Hodson in the *Esso* case).

(a) The parties' interests

The first limb of the test gave rise to a two-headed test of its own which will be considered in greater detail in later chapters: the covenantee must have a legitimate interest meriting protection and the protection must be no greater than necessary for the protection of that interest. As regards the interest meriting protection, a covenantee who has no such interest will never be given protection. A naked covenant can never be valid, as appears from *Vancouver Malt & Sake Brewing Co Ltd* v *Vancouver Breweries Ltd* (1934) in which the Privy Council declined to uphold a covenant in the purported sale of a licence to brew beer by which the vendors agreed not to compete in the brewing of beer for a period of fifteen years, on the grounds that the vendors had never in fact brewed beer and there was therefore no existing business to protect.

It is interesting to note that the courts have chosen to balance the interests of both parties, which at first sight clearly seem to be unequal. On the one hand it seems that, while a restraint will always be in the interests of the party it protects, on the other, it can hardly be in the interest of the party it restrains. Nevertheless, the courts have accepted that, even if undesirable, it is sometimes necessary for a party to accept a restraint in his own interest. A vendor of a business, it is said, would have difficulty selling that business if he refused to agree to any restraint on his right to compete with the buyer because, in the absence of any agreement to the contrary, he could simply set up again next door and carry on business as before (*Trego* v *Hunt* (1896)). Looked at from this angle, the inclusion of a restraint could therefore be in the vendor's interests. The courts have (perhaps with less success) sought to find justification for restraints in other cases. For example, it has been said that an employer would not pass on his skills and secrets to an employee if he could not restrain the employee from going to work for a rival. Such justifications will be examined later, but it is probably true to say that, in recent times, the courts have given up seeking to justify their upholding of a restraint and have simply accepted the view that, if the restraint is reasonable, justification in more general terms is irrelevant. In other words, the public interest has been subsumed into the parties' interests, which have in turn been swallowed up in the "no wider than is reasonably necessary" test.

(b) The public interest

The courts experience some difficulty in dealing with this aspect of the doctrine. As mentioned above, this has more often than not been taken to be commensurate with the general public policy rationale underpinning the doctrine. However, it is submitted that public interest with respect to a particular restraint is a much narrower concept than the public policy formulations considered under that heading earlier. As judges have occasionally pointed out, the loss of a person's business to the public in one geographical area will be of benefit to the public in the alternative area where he is forced to set up his business.

If the public policy in question is freedom to trade, then any restraint will be contrary to public policy. If public interest means the same thing, then the requirement is superfluous. A more logical formulation is to ask whether, although restraints generally are contrary to public policy, there might nevertheless be some more particular interest of the public in these special circumstances which allows deviation from what public policy generally requires. This, it is submitted, is what Lord Macnaghten's test means, but the courts have rarely taken this approach. Public interest is perhaps even more difficult to identify than public policy. It is therefore hardly surprising that courts have taken an easier route in modern times, paying mere lip service to this limb of the test while holding that if the restraint is reasonable with respect to the parties' interests then it must be reasonable in the public interest, and that the single test of reasonableness is that the restriction should not exceed what is necessary to protect the covenantee's legitimate interests.

(c) Reasonableness or fairness?

In *Schroeder Music Publishing Co Ltd* v *Macaulay* (1974) the plaintiff was a young, unpublished songwriter. He signed a standard form of agreement with the defendants, a music publishing company. Under the agreement, he assigned all the copyright in his works to the company, the defendants being under no obligation to publish any of the works. In return he was to be paid royalties on any published works and was given an advance of £50. The duration of the agreement was five years. It was held by the House of Lords that this contract was in restraint of trade.

Lord Diplock's remarks on public policy have already been noted above and have been taken by some commentators as possibly furthering the developing doctrine of economic duress (see for example *Law of Contract* (Butterworth, 11th edition, 1986) by Cheshire and Fifoot at pages 19, 20 and 276). Otherwise the fact that the restraint doctrine was successfully applied seems to have attracted little comment.

It is interesting to note how Lord Reid approaches the subject of reasonableness. Having stated that one could not reasonably expect a publisher to commit himself to publish songs written by an unknown songwriter, he continues:

> "... it appears to me to be an unreasonable restraint to tie the composer for this period of years so that his work will be sterilised and he can earn nothing *from his abilities as a composer* if the publisher chooses not to publish." (Author's italics.)

Lord Reid concludes that it is unreasonable. By what criterion is it unreasonable? The song-writer is given £50 − a not insignificant sum at that date − and the chance of having his songs published. Certainly, there was no "best endeavours" clause on the part of the publishers but if the songs the plaintiff wrote were of commercial value, presumably it would have been in the publisher's interests to exploit them. On the other hand, the plaintiff was apparently under no obligation to write songs for the defendants and could have carried on any other sort of trade – if an unpublished songwriter is in the "trade" of writing songs at all – and any songs he might have submitted (indeed there is no evidence in the report that he actually wrote any songs during the subsistence of the agreement) could have been valueless. The case has been taken to derive from the line of cases where, with reference to Lord Pearce's dicta mentioned earlier, the covenantor is unilaterally fettered and, to use Lord Reid's phrase, his work is sterilised. Yet it is inconsistent with another line of authority, beginning with *Lumley* v *Wagner* (1852) and including *Warner Bros Pictures Inc* v *Nelson* (1937) (see Chapter 11) where this type of contract has consistently been upheld, save where the covenantor was specifically restrained from earning his living in any other way (which was clearly not the case here). When they have read these cases, students might like to consider whether the position of Mr Macaulay, who could not write for anyone else, was so different from that of Miss Davis (in *Warner Bros*), who could not act for anyone else. True, the actress was in receipt of a salary, but she had no say as to whether she was to act at all. The songwriter on the other hand could at least partially control the situation by writing songs worthy of publication.

It is submitted that there is at least an arguable case that the agreement was reasonable in the interests of both parties. A further argument in its favour is that an unpublished songwriter could hardly have expected much more – indeed Lord Reid seems to have expected no positive commitment on the part of the publisher. Such restraints are not unusual in the business and, by analogy with business sales, he could probably not have got any agreement to publish his songs without such a restraint. Yet these arguments were not considered.

The only apparent concern of the court was that the defendants had used their superior bargaining position to impose a contract on the plaintiff which he might not otherwise have signed. Superior bargaining power has been considered a justification in the past for scrutinising restraints in contracts of employment rather than those in business sale agreements. Yet this was not a contract of employment and the restraints were not post-termination restraints; nor did they prevent the covenantor from earning his living in any other way.

It appears that although the judges used the word "reasonable", what they really meant was "fair". Something which is reasonable so far as particular parties are concerned may not be fair when judged by an objective standard. An unpublished songwriter should not have standard form restrictions imposed on him because a published songwriter would have been able to make his own contract. Naturally, but to apply the same test to both is to substitute an objective for a subjective test – perhaps a test of reasonableness in the public interest (although the judgments do not say this). It may be a good test; it may even be the right test, when viewed in the light of Lord Macnaghten's formulation, but it is not the *same* test, it is submitted, that the courts have grown accustomed to using in modern times. It remains to be seen whether this indicates a new development in the court's thinking on reasonableness in restraint of trade, but it does highlight one of the major problems of dealing with the doctrine: the principles to be applied may shift from time to time.

(d) Interpreting the clause

The courts have developed two rules to help them determine whether a clause is reasonable or not. These rules are considered in detail in Chapter 6. The first rule is familiar to all students of contract and is that the courts will construe the contract literally and any ambiguities are to be construed in the light of the document as a whole.

The second rule is known as the doctrine of severance and, although it does apply to other areas of contract, so many developments have occurred in its application to the restraint doctrine that it is identified as being a major part of that doctrine. Accordingly, it may be helpful at this point to say a few words by way of introduction to the concept of severance as it applies to restraint clauses.

A restraint may be partly reasonable and partly unreasonable; or there may be a number of restraint clauses in a single contract, some of which are reasonable, some unreasonable. If the unreasonable restraints can be removed from the contract leaving a contract which still makes sense, then the whole contract will not be avoided: the unreasonable restraints will simply be unenforceable. In *Goldsoll* v *Goldman* (1915) the defendant was the vendor of a business selling imitation jewellery in London. The sale agreement restrained the defendant for two years from dealing in "real or imitation" jewellery in any part of the United Kingdom or certain other countries listed in the agreement. The court held that restraining the defendant from selling imitation jewellery in the United Kingdom was reasonable, since he obtained most of his customers through advertising in national publications. The court therefore struck out the references to "real" jewellery and to countries other than the United Kingdom, and upheld the validity of the covenant as amended.

However, the court will not go so far as to make a new agreement for the parties; it will exercise its power of severance only where the restraint is effectively a combination of several distinct covenants. By way of contrast, in *Attwood* v *Lamont* (1920), the appellant had a department store in Kidderminster which contained drapery, tailoring and general outfitting departments. The respondent was head cutter and manager of the tailoring department but had nothing to do with the other departments. The covenant in question restrained him from carrying on the trades of "tailor, dressmaker, general draper, milliner, hatter, haberdasher, gentlemen's, ladies' or children's outfitter" in any place within ten miles of Kidderminster. The respondent left the appellant's business and set up business as a tailor within the prohibited area. The appellant argued that the covenant could be severed by deleting all trades other than that of tailor. The Court of Appeal, however, reversing the decision of the lower court, unanimously declined to do so. The specifying of a list of trades did no more than describe the whole business of the defendant and was unreasonable because the plaintiff was concerned only with tailoring.

The two cases are distinguishable on their facts, but a further reconciliation has been sought in the fact that one concerned the sale of a business and the other a contract of employment. As will become apparent later, the courts are more lenient towards employees than they are to sellers of businesses.

4. Alternatives to an express covenant

There has been a strong tendency for covenantees to abandon the restrictions under express covenants, if they think they may be too wide, and claim that the covenantor is in breach of some wider equitable principle. This is possible because in more recent times certain principles have developed to overlap with the area covered by the restraint doctrine and which afford the covenantee quite a wide degree of protection.

There are two wider equitable principles, sometimes overlapping, which have a bearing on the restraint of trade doctrine. These are the duties of good faith and confidentiality. Each will be discussed more fully in relation to specific types of agreement but for the moment two important effects on the doctrine may be noted:

(a) in the absence of an express contractual restraint, or if the covenantee chooses to abandon his rights under an express covenant, equitable principles may be invoked so as to have a restraining effect;

(b) if an express restraint goes no further than to spell out an equitable duty that the covenantor already owes, it is likely to be deemed reasonable.

However, it should not be forgotten that, provided it is reasonable, an express covenant can usually give greater protection to the covenantee than the equitable rules.

(a) Good faith

An employee owes his employer a duty of good faith which is implied into every contract of employment. The extent of this implied duty as it applies during the period of employment is very wide indeed and can be invoked to restrain an employee from taking on work for a competitor during his employment, even in the absence of any express restraint: *Hivac* v *Park Royal Scientific Instruments* (1946).

In *Hivac* the company was in the business of manufacturing valves for hearing aids. Some of its skilled employees undertook work for a rival organisation during their spare time. There was no provision in their contracts of employment prohibiting them from doing so, nor had the employees in question disclosed to their employer's rivals any confidential information or used any such information in their spare time employment. Nevertheless, undertaking such employment was held to be in breach of the duty of good faith implied into their contracts. It was the potential danger that confidential information might inadvertently or deliberately be revealed against which the employer was entitled to protection. However, the nature of the confidential information was not placed under scrutiny as it would have been in a restraint case.

The duty of good faith, although strictly enforced during the continuance of the contract of employment would seem not to have the same force once the contract has been terminated: *Faccenda Chicken Ltd* v *Fowler* (1986).

In *Faccenda Chicken*, the first defendant was employed as the plaintiff's sales manager. He was in charge of the sale of fresh chickens from refrigerated vans, the actual sales being carried out by a number of van salesmen. He then resigned and formed a rival company carrying on a similar business in the same area. Several of the plaintiff's van salesmen went to work for him. The defendant and the salesmen possessed information comprising the names and addresses of the plaintiff's customers, detailed routes, customers' requirements, times of deliveries and prices. The plaintiff claimed an injunction against the defendants and damages for breaches of contracts of employment and/or breach of confidence. None of the defendant's contracts with the plaintiff contained provisions prohibiting the unauthorised use of confidential information or trade secrets (ie, there were no restraint clauses whatsoever). The Court of Appeal held that:

(i) in the absence of express terms, an employee was bound by his implied duty of good faith not to disclose for the duration of his employment confidential information belonging to his employer; and

(ii) the duty continued after termination of the employment but only in relation to what could properly be described as a trade secret; there was no continuing duty in relation to confidential information not amounting to a trade secret; and

(iii) since the information in question did not amount to a trade secret, the employees were at liberty to use and disclose it as they thought fit.

The corollary, of course, is that if the information had amounted to a trade secret, the employees would have been restrained from using it, even after termination. The duty of confidentiality may then be commensurate with the permissible scope of a restraint on post-termination disclosure, but may not give protection where there has been no actual use or disclosure of the information. The question of whether or not the employee can be restrained from selling the information in the absence of a covenant was left open.

Where the employee is also a fiduciary, the duty will be more strict. An agent's duty of good faith, owed to his principal, has a number of facets: he must neither compete with his principal nor use the principal's property or confidential information in another business. Nor may he make a secret profit.

Partners are a special kind of agent, owing duties to one another and having a dual role as both agent and principal in respect of one another. Their duty of good faith appears to be more extensive than that of other agents. It arises from s 29(a) Partnership Act 1890 which says that:

> "Every partner must account to the firm for any benefit derived by him without the consent of the other partners from any transaction concerning the partnership, or from any use by him of the partnership property name or business connection".

Section 30 continues:

> "If a partner, without the consent of the other partners, carries on any business of the same nature as and competing with that of the firm, he must account for and pay over to the firm all profits made by him in that business."

However, s 30 applies only to a similar business. In *Aas* v *Benham* (1891) for example, a partner in a shipbroking firm started a ship-building company. It was held that he was in breach of neither s 29(a) nor s 30.

The implied duty may continue after the termination of the contract, but its extent is unclear. In *Floydd* v *Cheney* (1970) one partner in a firm of architects copied documents belonging to the firm while the other partner was away on vacation. When the other partner returned, the first terminated his agreement, intending to use the copy documents in his own new business. The court held he was in breach of duty and must return the documents. It is to be noted, however, that his wrongdoing began while he was still a partner, since it was done with the intention of setting up in competition (bad faith). The conclusion might have been different if the partner had merely used information which he had innocently retained in his head.

A company director, as an agent, also owes a duty of good faith to his principal, the company. In *Industrial Development Consultants Ltd* v *Cooley* (1972) a director was negotiating a contract with a potential customer of his company. The other party indicated that they were not prepared to award the contract to the company but would award it to the director personally if he would leave the company and set up his own business. He did so and the court held that he was in breach of his fiduciary duty and must account to the company for all profits received from the contract.

Again it is to be noted that, while the judgment applied to a post-termination business, the real act of bad faith began while the defendant was still a director. The fiduciary duty of a director is certainly not as extensive as that of a partner, however, and directors may be involved in a competing business during the period of their directorship (see further Chapter 4).

(b) Confidentiality

As can be seen from *Faccenda Chicken Ltd* v *Fowler*, there is often an overlap between the duties of good faith and confidentiality, but every breach of confidentiality is not always a breach of good faith (as decided in *Faccenda Chicken* itself), and breaches of good faith by no means always involve breaches of confidentiality.

The duty of confidentiality extends over a wide area and includes information gained not only in an employer-employee relationship but also in a whole range of situations, many of which also fall within the restraint doctrine. For example, a franchisee will often have imparted to him details of a secret process involved in the franchise; or a patent licensee may be licensed to use certain confidential information relating to the patent. Usually there will be express covenants in the agreements regulating the use of any confidential information, and restrictions are likely to fall within the restraint of trade doctrine. It should, however, be noted that only confidential information amounting to a trade secret can form the basis of a reasonable restraint clause.

In the absence of express covenants, the court will nevertheless step in to prevent unauthorised use or disclosure of the information provided that the requirements of breach of confidence are satisfied. The interface between the doctrines of restraint of trade and confidentiality may raise problems of interpretation. Consider the two following cases.

Torrington Manufacturing v *Smith & Sons* (1966) concerned a licensing agreement for the manufacture of fans with the use of the licensor's patents and designs. It contained a provision to the effect that in the event of the licensor determining the agreement, the licensee could retain the right to use the licensor's confidential information in the manufacture of fans "the subject of the licensor's patents and registered designs". However, the licensee wished to use the information to manufacture fans which were not the subject of the licensor's patents or registered designs. It was held that, since the agreement was silent on the point, it fell to be decided under the general equitable principles relating to confidence which restrained the licensee from using the confidential information for this other purpose.

In *Regina Glass Fibre* v *Schuller* (1972) the agreement was also a licensing agreement which concerned a patent and certain confidential information. The agreement had expired by effluxion of time and the question was whether the licensee could use confidential information relating to improvements which the licensor had communicated to him during the contractual period. The agreement contained a provision which expressly entitled the licensee during the contractual period to require the licensor to grant them exclusive rights to the use of improvements. Here it was held that the clause could be deemed to continue after the termination of the agreement so as to allow the licensee to use the improvement, although the court thought this could not have been what the parties intended.

The lesson to be learned from these two cases is that the boundary between contractual restraints and breach of confidence is a grey area, and if express provision is not made for all foreseeable eventualities, the court may fill the lacunae in ways which the parties might not have intended.

5. Types of confidential information

In a number of cases, the courts have considered different types of information and the protection to be afforded to each. It has already been shown how in *Faccenda Chicken Ltd* v *Fowler* trade secrets were afforded a greater measure of implied protection than other confidential information.

In *Morris* v *Saxelby* (see page 8) Lord Shaw drew a distinction between information the use of which could be restrained and other information:

> "Trade secrets, the names of customers – all such things which in sound philosophical language are denominated objective knowledge – these may not be given away by a servant; they are his master's property and there is no rule of public interest which prevents transfer of them against his master's will being restrained. On the other hand, a man's aptitudes, his skill, his dexterity, his manual or mental ability – all those things which in sound philosophical language are not objective but subjective – they may and ought not to be relinquished by a servant; they are not his master's property – they are his own property; they are himself".

(a) Trade secrets

It is not always clear what is meant by a "trade secret". The term was originally used in Victorian cases to mean technological manufacturing information. Yet while statute and case law alike continue to use the term, they provide no precise definition, and the words usually precede the phrase "and other confidential information". In *Thomas Marshall (Exports) Ltd* v *Guinle* (1979), which concerned an attempt to restrain an ex-managing director from disclosing and using information gained in his employment, Sir Robert Megarry VC made no distinction between the two terms: "Costs and prices which are not generally known may well constitute trade secrets or confidential information".

Yet it is clear not only that "confidential information" bears a wider meaning but, since the decision in *Faccenda Chicken*, it appears that the general principle of confidentiality may differ in its application depending on whether or not the information amounts to a trade secret. In *Faccenda Chicken* it was necessary to the judgment to distinguish between trade secrets and other confidential information, but the judges were reluctant to undertake the task of defining the term with precision and instead spoke somewhat vaguely about degrees of confidentiality. At first instance, Goulding J classified confidential information into three types varying by degree of confidentiality. Into the third category fell specific trade secrets which were so confidential that, even though the employee had memorised them rather than copied them, they could not lawfully be used to benefit anyone other than the employer, even after termination of the employment contract.

Delivering the judgment of the Court of Appeal, Neill LJ spoke of the impossibility of listing those things which could be deemed to qualify as trade secrets or confidential information equivalent to a trade secret. He gave as an example secret manufacturing processes; this is such an obvious example of a trade secret that it is not a very useful one. He admitted that there were innumerable other pieces of confidential information, the confidentiality of which would be short lived (it is not clear from the judgment whether he thought they could be protected or not, but he was probably implying that they could), but he gave no examples.

This attitude is not particularly helpful to the lawyer or businessman struggling to ascertain which information may be protected as a trade secret. There are probably any number of pieces of information which the businessman might regard as being so confidential that it would cause damage to his business if any of them were to be revealed to a rival. Nevertheless, it is only in *Thomas Marshall (Exports) Ltd* v *Guinle* that any test giving substantial weight to the views of the owner of the information has been proposed.

(b) Know-how

The term "know-how" is widely used in agreements and has received recognition in a number of statutes. In the Income and Corporation Taxes Act 1970, for example, it is defined for the purposes of s 386 as " ... any industrial information and techniques likely to assist in the manufacture or processing of goods or materials, or in the working of a mine, oil-well or other source of mineral deposits (including the searching for, discovery, or testing of deposits or the winning of access thereto), or in the carrying out of any agricultural, forestry or fishing operations".

"Know-how" seems to straddle the border of the distinction drawn by Lord Shaw in *Morris* v *Saxelby* since it may comprise both information imparted by an employer or licensor and elements of the employee's or licensee's own skill which has led to the discovery of certain techniques for himself. Suffice it to say for the time being that it may be difficult to distinguish between skill belonging to the employee and know-how belonging to his employer.

(c) Lists of names and addresses

An ex-employee may have in his possession lists of names and addresses and other information relating to customers and other employees of his former employer. These could well be of assistance to him in setting up a competing business or could be of value to his new employer.

In *Robb* v *Green* (1895) the plaintiff sold game birds to country gentlemen. The defendant, who was the plaintiff's former manager, copied a list of the names and addresses of the plaintiff's customers and later, having left his employment with the plaintiff, solicited business from them for his own competing concern. It was held that this information was confidential and the defendant could be restrained by injunction from using it. The decision in *Faccenda Chicken* however, casts doubt upon the proposition that use of a former employer's list of customers and similar information will, in the absence of an express contractual restraint, be restrained for breach of confidentiality; but it should be noted that the Court of Appeal in *Faccenda Chicken* did not expressly overrule *Robb* v *Green* or other similar cases which were cited to it.

The employee might not steal or copy written or printed lists of customers but may simply have them inside his head, either because he had taken the trouble to memorise them or because he cannot help remembering them. In *Coral Index* v *Regent Index* (1970) the plaintiff's business was a gambling concern whereby his customers could bet on the Financial Times Index going up or down. The plaintiff's former office manager left the business and solicited the plaintiff's customers for a competing concern. The court drew a distinction between deliberate and involuntary committal to memory, and held that as this case concerned the latter it should fail at the interlocutory stage. This suggests that the court is not so much concerned with the duty of confidentiality but with a pre-termination breach of good faith having post-termination effects. In *Robb* v *Green* there was bad faith, but in both *Faccenda Chicken* and *Coral Index* there was no indication that the employee had exercised bad faith *while he was an employee*.

A further possibility is that the employee may have information not about customers but about other employees which might be extremely valuable to rival employers mounting a "head-hunting" operation. In *GD Searle & Co* v *Celltech* (1982) an ex-employee of the plaintiff's possessed information concerning research scientists employed by the plaintiffs including names, characters, aptitudes and specialisations. This information, it was alleged, would have been of considerable use to a rival company and the plaintiffs sought to restrain disclosure. The court held that it was not inequitable for competitors to seek out and offer employment to employees of a rival concern, provided that they did not actually procure a breach of the employees' contracts, and the use of such information could not therefore be restrained.

(d) Other confidential information

In order to obtain any protection from equity or under the restraint doctrine, the information must be in the nature of confidential information. In *Thomas Marshall (Exports)* v *Guinle*, Sir Robert Megarry VC proposed a new test of confidentiality. Information would be confidential if it satisfied all the following four requirements:

(i) the owner of the information must believe that the release of the information would be injurious to him or advantageous to his rivals or others;

(ii) the owner must believe that the information is confidential or secret (ie, not already in the public domain);

(iii) the owner's belief in (i) and (ii) must be reasonable;

(iv) the information must be judged in the light of the usage and practices of the particular industry or trade concerned.

Note that it is the owner's belief which is important, but it must be judged objectively in the light of trade practice and usage. This, it is submitted, is a good test in so far as the owner's views must be relevant and ought not to be ignored as has been the case in the past. Yet it begs the question whether the employee should be restrained from disclosing information which he does not know or believe to be confidential. Perhaps it would be unjust to judge the matter purely from the owner's point of view since the recipient of the information will usually have no choice, if he is an employee, in whether or not it is given to him. In these circumstances, the court ought surely not to award damages for innocent use or disclosure, or restrain the recipient on that basis from setting up his own business or working for a competitor.

It has already been noted that different degrees of confidentiality engender different degrees of protection and it may be useful to conclude by identifying the two lower classes of information distinguished by Goulding J in *Faccenda Chicken*. These comprise:

(i) information which is trivial in nature or is in the public domain and easily accessible;

(ii) information which an employee knows to be confidential because he is told so, or ought to know is confidential because of its character, and which, due to his using it in the performance of his duties for the employer, he remembers so that it becomes part of his knowledge and skill.

The first category of information in the judge's view carries no duty to keep it confidential, even while the employee is in the employment to which it relates. In fact it is not to be regarded as confidential at all. Disclosure of the second category is restrained only so long as the employment continues. Afterwards he may use it as he wishes. The use of this kind of information might, however, be restrained under the *Guinle* test (but the strict *ratio* of *Guinle* deals only with restraint during employment and therefore the judgments are not incompatible).

As *Faccenda Chicken* was concerned with implied duties, it is not clear how far this categorisation applies to contractual restraints, but it appears that Goulding J thought the second category could be protected by a restraint clause. (See further Chapter 3.)

6. Breach of confidence

For a breach of confidence action to succeed, three things must be shown (*Coco* v *AN Clark (Engineers)* (1968)):

(a) the information must have the "necessary quality of confidence" about it (see above);

(b) it must have been imparted in circumstances importing an obligation of confidence; and

(c) there must be an unauthorised use of the information to the detriment of the party communicating it.

One other distinction between an action for breach of confidence and an action for breach of a restraint clause is immediately clear. In the former, both unauthorised use and detriment must be shown. In the latter, the defendant may be restrained without proof of either.

Sometimes it may be impossible for the owner to sue the party to whom he communicated the information, or the information may have already been disclosed so that it is third parties who must be restrained from disclosing it further. Here, breach of confidence scores over breach of contract. There is ample evidence in the case law that the owner of confidential information may restrain a third party to whom it is unlawfully communicated from publishing or otherwise using it. However, this has usually concerned third parties who were perfectly well aware that the information was confidential. Where the third party is innocent, the court might prove reluctant to impose a duty of confidence on him. Clearly there is a "chain of duty" where the third party knows that the information was confidential and that the intermediary had no right to reveal it. It is likely also that the duty will extend to the third party where he ought reasonably to have appreciated that the information was communicated to him in breach of confidence. However there are dicta in some cases (*Morison* v *Moat* (1852) and *Stevenson Jordan & Harrison* v *Macdonald & Evans* (1952)) to suggest that the court might take a more lenient view if the circumstances were otherwise. The point is a moot one, as there are dicta in *Fraser* v *Evans* (1968) which suggest that even if the third party came by the information innocently he might still be restrained from breaking the confidence once he knew it to be confidential.

For present purposes, the point is that it is probably unwise for the owner of confidential information to take the risk, and some express provision should be made where possible for indemnifying the owner against the consequences of disclosure, whoever might be the actual publisher of the information.

7. Conclusions

This short summary of the scope of the doctrine and its alternatives has sought to highlight some important points to be borne in mind by the practitioner when drafting or evaluating potential restraints. These can be briefly summarised by way of conclusion:

- All restraints of trade are void unless reasonable.

- The courts may examine any type of contract, and although some restraints − pure negative restrictive covenants attached to land, for instance − are likely to be outside the ambit of the doctrine, they nevertheless need to be worded carefully to secure immunity.

- The doctrine is founded on public policy, and public policy may change. It may be used as an instrument to strike down a bargain which the court considers unconscionable.

- Validation of a clause requires that it be reasonable in scope, duration and its geographical limits.

- Reasonable means reasonable both in the interests of the parties and in the public interest. The court's attitude to these requirements has varied from time to time and it is not always clear whether a restraint is required to satisfy a subjective test, an objective test, or both.

- If a restraint is found to be unreasonable, the whole contract is void, but if the contract is workable without the restraint, only the restraint will be unenforceable.

- If there are a number of independent restraints and only some are unreasonable, or if a restraint is only partly unreasonable, provided the reasonable part or parts can be interpreted as a separate covenant and the rest can stand independently of the unreasonable parts, the reasonable parts may be enforceable.

- The courts' approach to interpretation has varied. They may strictly interpret the wording of a clause or they may use a more liberal approach.

- Although the cases are mainly concerned with restraints which subsist after the termination of an agreement, the courts may concern themselves with restraints which exist during the currency of the agreement.

- Equitable remedies exist, particularly breach of confidence and good faith, to restrain certain activities even where there is no express covenant governing them; the courts may take the equitable principles into consideration when evaluating a restraint and it will usually be held good if it does not exceed the limits of the equitable protection.

- Nevertheless, it is unsafe to leave the matter to be governed by implied covenants, as the courts are likely to afford greater protection under an express covenant, provided that it is reasonable.

- A covenant stated to be for the duration of the agreement might be impliedly extended to cover the period after termination, but, if not, the protection after termination will be no more than that given by general equitable principles.

Chapter 2

Protecting a business sale agreement

In *Trego* v *Hunt* (1896), the court held that the vendor of a business could set up a similar business, even using the same name, anywhere he chose, notwithstanding that it would cause considerable damage to the goodwill he had just sold. The case concerned the sale of goodwill of a partnership on dissolution but has been taken to provide the basic rule for business sales generally. It demonstrates at its most liberal the *laissez-faire* attitude to freedom to trade. It seems improbable that the decision would be repeated in the modern economic climate but it remains with us, highlighting the vital need for restraints on competition in contracts for the sale of a business.

In *Nordenfelt* v *Maxim Nordenfelt Guns and Ammunition Co* (1894), an armaments manufacturer sold his business to a company under an agreement containing certain restraint clauses. Later, there was a merger between this company and another, and the merged company agreed to employ the former owner as its managing director under a service agreement containing similar restraints. This particular landmark in the history of restraint clauses is notable for a number of things but in this context it is worth citing for the liberal view taken by the House of Lords in upholding a worldwide, effectively lifelong restraint contained in the two agreements, on the ground that the company had a legitimate interest worthy of protection in the goodwill of the business which, as it happened, extended throughout the world. This opened the way to a more favourable consideration of restraints in connection with contracts for the sale of a business.

Trego v *Hunt* and the *Nordenfelt* case seem to represent opposite poles of Victorian thinking: freedom of trade being paramount in the former and freedom of contract in the latter. However, they can be synthesised into the principle governing business sales which has guided the courts ever since: if the purchaser places no restraints on the seller's future conduct, it may be taken that the seller can do whatever he chooses so long as he does not actively solicit his former customers. If, on the other hand, the purchaser seeks to restrain the seller by provisions in the sale agreement, he should be allowed to do so, provided that (a) the restrictions are not naked restraints on competition, and (b) the restraint does not extend further than the actual business sold.

Thus, in relation to business sale agreements, the question of whether there is an interest meriting protection is of paramount importance. The determination of whether or not a restraint is reasonable in terms of its duration or its geographical area is therefore of correspondingly less importance (although this does not mean that a restriction may not be struck down if it seeks to protect a geographical area much greater than is necessary).

1. The goodwill of the business

The rationale of the courts' liberal approach to restraints in business sale agreements is clearly apparent from the following dictum of James VC in *Leather Cloth Co* v *Lorsont* (1869), which has been cited with approval in the higher courts more than once:

> "... public policy requires that when a man has by skill or by any other means obtained something which he wants to sell, he should be at liberty to sell it in the most advantageous way in the market; and in order to enable him to sell it advantageously in the market it is necessary that he should be able to preclude himself from entering into competition with the purchaser."

In the case of such a sale of property, ie a business, public policy requires that he can protect himself by provisions in the contract of sale, however restrictive, provided that, taking into consideration the subject-matter of the contract, the court does not consider the restrictions to be unreasonable.

Lord Atkinson in the later case of *Morris* v *Saxelby* considered that the sale of the goodwill of a business is to be distinguished from other cases, especially that of a contract of employment, because the covenant enhances the value of the contract.

Lord Parker was equally convinced of this. Refusing to accept the argument that there was no distinction to be drawn between the position of the purchaser of the goodwill of a business taking a covenant from his vendor and the case of the owner of a business taking such a covenant from his servant or apprentice, he explained that the distinction had been recognised in *Nordenfelt* v *Maxim Nordenfelt Guns and Ammunition Co* by both Lord Macnaghten and Lord Herschell. The purchaser of a business, said Lord Parker, is entitled to have the goodwill kept immune from competition by the vendor. If this were not the case, the purchaser would not be getting what he had contracted to buy and the vendor would not be giving what he had contracted to sell.

Lord Shaw in *Mason* v *Provident Clothing and Supply Co Ltd* (1913), although perhaps more cautious as to the actual circumstances, was convinced that restraints in business sale agreements would be upheld in law at least in the following circumstances:

> "It may clearly appear that the express view of the bargain may have been the elimination from the sphere of competition of the powerful personality of a possible rival who by the very terms of the contract had been paid for disappearing into retirement, carrying his sheaves with him."

Goodwill, then, is the interest meriting protection. It has been defined by the courts in a number of ways, all of them imprecise. Lord Macnaghten in *Trego* v *Hunt* [1896] AC 7 defines it at page 24 as:

> "the whole advantage, whatever it may be, of the reputation and connection of the firm which may have been built up by years of honest work or gained by lavish expenditure of money".

In *Hill* v *Fearis* [1905] 1 Ch 466, Warrington J explains at page 471 that goodwill is:

> "the advantage, whatever it may be, which a person gets by continuing to carry on, and being entitled to represent to the outside world that he is carrying on, a business which has been carried on for some time previously".

However in *Crutwell* v *Lye* (1810) 17 Ves 335 at page 346, Lord Eldon puts it no higher than "the probability of the old customers resorting to the old place".

Nevertheless, it has a value, and is implied in a business sale, whether specifically referred to in the agreement or not (*Shipwright* v *Clements* (1871)), and the price paid by the purchaser is what entitles him to protect it. As *Trego* v *Hunt* itself illustrated, the value of the goodwill sold is nullified if the vendor, possibly the worst rival the purchaser could have, were simply to set up business again in the same area, for the likelihood is that his former customers, whether through desire, habit or confusion, would continue to patronise him, rather than go to his purchaser. A covenant is upheld simply because it can be invoked to prevent that.

Therefore, the vendor can and should protect the goodwill of his new business by a covenant in restraint. However, even given the courts' liberal attitude to such covenants, it must still not go further than protecting what the purchaser has bought. The question is, what degree of protection will be deemed reasonable enough to validate the covenant. In *British Reinforced Concrete Engineering Co Ltd* v *Schelff* (1921), the defendants were sellers of "loop" road reinforcements while the plaintiffs manufactured and sold "BRC" road reinforcements. The contract for sale of the defendants' business to the plaintiffs contained a clause preventing the defendants from competing with the plaintiffs in the manufacture and sale of "road reinforcements". Since this went beyond the "loop" road reinforcements business actually being sold, it was held to be too wide and therefore void. (It is to be noted that the courts were not prepared to interpret the restriction as applying only to "loop" road reinforcements.)

Reasonableness in relation to a restraint taken by the purchaser of a business is therefore to be judged by the extent and circumstances of the business sold, not by any business of the purchaser of which, after transfer, the business sold will form part.

In *Giblin* v *Murdoch* (1979), a slightly different point arose. The purchaser of a gentlemen's hairdressing business had taken a covenant from his vendor. The question was, could he enforce it when the vendor had set up as a ladies' hairdresser. The answer was that he could not. Therefore it appears that, however liberal the courts' approach in general, in this it is very strict indeed.

The recent case of *Systems Reliability Holdings plc* v *Smith* (1990) gives us an interesting insight into the High Court's current thinking on restraints in business sale agreements. The defendant was employed by a company (ECS) in a highly skilled technical position modifying computer hardware, and, during his employment, purchased shares amounting to 1.6 per cent of the total issued share capital of the company. He was dismissed from his employment and ECS was subsequently taken over by the plaintiff company. The defendant, together with the other shareholders (who were still within ECS), sold his shares to the plaintiffs. The sale agreement, which the defendant had approved in draft (without taking legal advice, although he had been advised by the purchasers to do so), contained several restrictive covenants by the "specifically restricted vendors" (including the defendant) for the benefit of the plaintiff company:

(a) not during the "restrictive period" (effectively seventeen months) directly or indirectly to carry on or be engaged or interested in any business competing with any business carried on at the date of the agreement by ECS or any of its subsidiaries (a non-competition covenant);

(b) not directly or indirectly to solicit the custom of any person who within the preceding two years was a customer of ECS or any of its subsidiaries (a non-solicitation covenant);

(c) not at any time after the date of the agreement to disclose or use for his own benefit or that of any other person any confidential information of ECS or any of its subsidiaries (a confidentiality covenant).

The defendant was employed, after his dismissal, by a competitor, but was dismissed from this position at the plaintiff's insistence. He then set up his own business and canvassed the custom of several competitors of ECS. The plaintiffs sought to enforce the restrictions by injunction.

The defendant put forward a number of arguments, and it is interesting to see how Harman J dealt with them. Firstly, the defendant said, this was an attempt to get an employer-employee covenant, not a vendor-purchaser restraint, and the restrictions should be judged by the stricter standards applicable to employer-employee contracts. The judge indicated that although it might be convenient, he did not find it helpful to observe the strict categories, and the proper question to be answered was: "What is reasonable in this particular deal?"

Secondly, the defendant argued that the goodwill belonged to the company and not to the shareholders, so that they could not be bound as vendors, and as the defendant held only 1.6 per cent of the equity he could not properly be regarded as a vendor of goodwill. Harman J rejected both arguments. By analogy with *Bridge* v *Deacons* (1984) (see Chapter 4), he found that, if ECS had been a partnership, it would have been possible to enforce the restrictive covenants against a partner holding only 1.6 per cent of the goodwill. The distinction between a company and a partnership in his view, was merely one of legal structure and that should not affect the case.

Thirdly, the defendant argued that the restrictions applied to other shareholders who held no confidential information of the company and were most unlikely ever to compete with it. The judge considered that the unenforceability of the covenant against some of the vendors did not mean that it could not be upheld against others against whom it was reasonable to enforce it.

Finally, the defendant submitted that the covenant was unreasonably wide as it purported to afford protection to the subsidiaries of ECS when the defendant was employed only by ECS itself. Of this, the judge said that it was not *prima facie* unreasonable and in the absence of evidence to show that it was unreasonable, there was nothing to prevent the court enforcing it if it was otherwise properly limited. In holding that it *was* otherwise properly limited, Harman J found that the worldwide restriction was reasonable in this case as the business was completely international and the duration comparatively limited.

A similarly liberal approach to a borderline covenant can be seen in *Allied Dunbar (Frank Weisinger) Ltd* v *Frank Weisinger* (1988). Here, the defendant was a self-employed sales associate of the financial services organisation, Allied Dunbar Assurance plc. The latter bought out his practice through its subsidiary, the plaintiff company, a company formed for that particular purpose. The sale agreement, which included goodwill and connection, provided that the defendant would be employed as a consultant by the company for a minimum period of two years. The agreement also contained a non-solicitation covenant and a non-competition covenant, which would, if upheld, effectively debar the defendant from working within the financial services industry in the United Kingdom for two years following termination of his consultancy agreement. The idea behind these practice buyouts, of which this was the first of a series, was that sales associates would be able to retire and the value of the practice would be maintained, having been realised for their benefit. The defendant had a number of years to go before reaching retiring age and, in his case, the consultancy arrangement was unsuccessful and was terminated by mutual agreement shortly after the buyout. The plaintiff company, learning that the defendant was about to take up employment with another financial services group, sought an injunction to restrain the defendant.

The defendant offered a number of undertakings aimed at mitigating the effect of his taking other employment. He undertook to comply with the non-solicitation covenant and, when this did not satisfy the plaintiffs, undertook to refuse to deal with any former clients who consulted him of their own accord and refer them back to the plaintiffs. He also offered payments in respect of any business he might acquire as a result of the recommendation of his former clients. None of these satisfied the plaintiffs, who contended they could only be protected by the strict terms of the non-competition covenant because they were entitled to be protected, not merely in respect of the existing clientele, but in respect of any new business which might accrue to the company as a result of its existing goodwill.

Miller J, looking at the substance rather than the form of the agreement, had no difficulty accepting that the covenants fell into the vendor-purchaser category, notwithstanding the consultancy agreement. Yet he, too, did not consider it was "a mere matter of categorisation" and thought the covenants might serve a dual purpose. The defendant based his argument on the ground that a non-competition covenant went too far in that it covered new clients not existing at the date of the agreement. The attraction of future clients, it was argued, depended on the quality of the service offered by the new owners and not the existing goodwill. In holding that this submission was incorrect and that the plaintiffs had a legitimate interest in trying to secure such new clients as might be referred or recommended to them, Miller J said:

"... the value of goodwill does not depend upon the prospect of clients acting rationally but upon the commercial expectation, based upon everyday experience, that some of them will not."

He added by way of illustration that people will return to or recommend a restaurant to others even though they know that it has a different chef and even though it is irrational for them to do so, an attitude towards customer behaviour which seems prevalent in the thinking of judges today and is discussed in the context of contracts of employment in Chapter 3.

He concluded that the plaintiffs were entitled, by virtue of the consideration paid, to the protection of a non-competition covenant which did not depend, as an undertaking or a non-dealing covenant would have done, on the vendor's honesty and co-operation, and further decided that, since Mr Weisinger had agreed to the restriction at the time of sale, it was not proper for him to challenge it at this later stage.

The liberal attitude to restraints in business sale agreements has clearly been extended, in present times, to hybrid agreements where the agreement involves at least an element of business sale. Nevertheless, one can argue with greater confidence that the decision was justified in *Frank Weisinger* than is possible in relation to *Systems Reliability* v *Smith*. In the latter case, the commercial reality was surely that the vendors were obtaining an employer-employee restriction based on the possession of trade secrets without the question of whether there were in fact any trade secrets being thoroughly considered, as it would surely have been in an employer-employee case. Had these been decided as employer-employee cases, the attitude taken by the courts might be gleaned by comparing with *Frank Weisinger* the case of *Lucas (T) & Co Ltd* v *Mitchell* (1972), and with *Systems Reliability* v *Smith* the case of *Balston Ltd* v *Headline Filters Ltd* (1990) in Chapters 3 and 4 respectively.

A non-solicitation covenant, unlike a non-dealing or non-competition covenant, will usually be held to be reasonable in relation to a business sale on the ground of legitimate interest and, even in the absence of an express covenant, the court will imply one (*Trego* v *Hunt*). It is not clear, however, how wide a covenant the court will imply. Therefore, as far as the draftsman is concerned, it is better to insert an express covenant which will stand a good chance of being upheld.

On the question of geographical area and duration, the rules and guidelines are roughly the same as those in employment and other contracts (these are explained in Chapter 6) but, as a general rule, more latitude is allowed in business sale agreements, and the view of Miller J in *Allied Dunbar* v *Frank Weisinger* that the parties themselves are, in this instance, the best judges of what is reasonable, is not an uncommon one. Nor, it is submitted, is this an unreasonable view to take. The parties are usually on an equal footing, are legally advised and have the opportunity of fully negotiating the terms. If, in that situation, they agree to restraints which they later come to consider unreasonable, they surely have only themselves or their legal advisers to blame.

2. Confidential information

It is often the case that the sale of a business will include trade secrets or other confidential information, know-how etc. There are fewer cases in this area but in *Hagg* v *Darley* (1878) a covenant on the sale of a disinfectant manufacturing business restraining the vendor from disclosing trade secrets was held to be valid, and it seems clear that the courts will not apply the stringent tests of confidentiality that they apply to information possessed by employees.

The likelihood of confidential information being involved is stronger, however, in borderline cases such as *Systems Reliability Holdings plc* v *Smith* where it is really a case of an employee selling shares rather than the usual form of business sale. The question here is whether this case will apply wherever an employee sells his shares on termination of his employment or only when there is a takeover of the whole issued capital. With employee share ownership becoming widespread and many employees holding shares otherwise than under special employee share schemes, the question is not unimportant. If the courts take the attitude to restraints that was taken in *Systems Reliability Holdings*, it could have fundamental implications for the application of the doctrine to employees.

In addition to the points noted above, the case demonstrates a novel approach to confidential information. It will be recalled that the agreement in question contained a confidentiality covenant. Harman J found that he was not bound by remarks in the Court of Appeal in *Faccenda Chicken* v *Fowler* (referred to in Chapter 1) to the effect that confidential information which did not amount to a trade secret could not be protected by an express covenant in restraint, since that case concerned an implied covenant of good faith which did not extend beyond termination. Nor did he feel bound to follow the decision of Cross J in *Printers and Finishers Ltd* v *Holloway* (1964) on the question of what amounted to confidential information which could receive protection from an express covenant, because, although concerned with confidentiality, it was also concerned with the implied duty and was a "true master and servant" case. Holding that in relation to a business sale, use and disclosure were both protectable by an express covenant, he was quite sure that it was a vendor-purchaser covenant which was before him for consideration, taken to protect the information which was a part of what the purchaser had bought. Accordingly he saw no problem in applying a more liberal test to it than he would have done had he been considering an employer-employee covenant.

In reaching his decision that the restriction was reasonable, the judge was influenced by the fact that the defendant knew at least some of the information he possessed was confidential, and the judge also took into consideration the fact that competitors had been allowed to watch the defendant performing certain operations from which, being skilled people, they might obtain the requisite know-how.

The courts have consistently declined to protect know-how under employment contracts. If the *Systems Reliability Holdings* case marks a new judicial approach to share sale and shareholders' agreements entered into by employees, it may mean a radical change in how courts assess "trade secrets" and, perhaps, in how employers frame their restrictions.

3. Trade name

The question has sometimes arisen whether the vendor of a business can trade under the name of the old business. The rules established from *Trego* v *Hunt* seem to allow it, but from *Boorne* v *Wicker* (1927) and *Curl Bros Ltd* v *Webster* (1904) it seems that a partner, after dissolution of the partnership, is not entitled to use the old firm name for his new business. There therefore seems to be some doubt on the true position. In *Vernon* v *Hallam* (1886), however, a covenant by a vendor not to trade under a particular name was held not to be in restraint of trade. The answer for the practitioner then seems to be to ensure that the agreement contains such a covenant.

4. Conclusions

The following points need to be borne in mind in connection with business sale agreements:

- A non-competition covenant will not be implied by the courts.
- A non-solicitation covenant *will* be implied but since the extent is not clear it should probably be backed up by express non-competition, non-dealing and non-solicitation covenants in the agreement.
- Express covenants are more readily upheld than those in employment contracts.
- The covenantee must show an interest meriting protection which may be goodwill or confidential information, but the extent of protection is in some cases wider than that afforded to employers.
- The covenant should not extend beyond the business purchased, even to cover the purchaser's existing business,

but may be allowed to include subsidiaries of the business purchased if not *prima facie* unreasonable.

- The court may examine the geographical area and duration but unless these are clearly unreasonable (eg, nationwide protection for a business operating in only a small locality) they will usually be upheld.

- In deciding how to approach "hybrid" agreements, the courts will not necessarily categorise them and will in any event look to the substance of the transaction.

Chapter 3

Protecting an employer

The courts' attitude towards restraints in contracts of employment is said to tend towards favouring the employee. According to this theory, such restraints are to be construed more strictly than those in other contracts. The House of Lords made its policy clear in *Morris* v *Saxelby*. In Lord Atkinson's judgment, if a restriction in an employee's contract were oppressive in the sense that it would, if enforced, prevent him for a considerable period from using the mechanical and technical skill and knowledge that he had obtained by means of his own industry, observation and intelligence, then it would be of concern to the public at large since it is in the public interest that he be free to exercise his skill and knowledge for the benefit of his employers.

In the *Nordenfelt* case, twenty years earlier, Lord Macnaghten had expressed the opinion that contracts between employer and employee should be distinguished from others on the ground that employees lacked the freedom to contract that, for example, the buyer of a business has. This is probably even more the case in modern times when it is common practice to offer an employee a standard form of contract of employment on a "take-it-or-leave-it" basis. While the employer will usually have taken legal advice on the contract, most employees, for reasons of cost if nothing else, will be unlikely to employ a solicitor to examine it from their point of view, and even if they were to do so, it is unlikely that the employer would be prepared to negotiate the restrictions in question. Lord Macnaghten's dictum should therefore still hold good when it comes to protecting an employee from the unreasonable anti-competitive desires of his employer. The importance which the courts have attached to disparity in bargaining power in modern times can be seen from *Schroeder Music Publishing Co* v *Macaulay* (discussed in Chapter 1) which, although not a case on contracts of employment, may indicate a general trend in judicial thought.

However, it should not be thought that the courts will allow no restraints in employment contracts. The theory is that they will subject them to more careful scrutiny and will apply, apparently more strictly, the tests of whether there is a legitimate interest meriting protection and whether the protection is wider than necessary to be reasonable. Since the element of reasonable protection has similar implications for all types of restraint, it is considered in isolation in Chapter 6. This chapter concerns the specific interests of an employer which are deemed to merit protection by means of a restraint clause.

In *Morris* v *Saxelby*, Lord Atkinson stated categorically that an employer was entitled to protect his trade secrets from being divulged and his customers from being solicited or enticed away. Although it does not appear in the judgment that these are the only interests capable of protection, the courts have since shown no inclination to extend these categories and it is clear that the employer who tries to impose restraints aimed at protecting other aspects of his business will fail. Argument has therefore concentrated on the nature of a trade secret or whether the employee may be deemed to have a customer connection.

1. Trade secrets

An express covenant in a contract of employment aimed at protecting trade secrets and other confidential information may take one or more of the following forms:

    (a) a restraint on use/disclosure of confidential information during the course of the employee's employment;

    (b) a restraint on use/disclosure of confidential information expressed to continue after termination of the employment;

    (c) a non-competition covenant expressly or impliedly justified with reference to confidential information of the employer which the employee may possess, expressed to be for the duration of the employment;

    (d) a non-competition covenant taken for a similar reason and expressed to be for a period following termination of the employment.

With regard to (a), the courts will not subject this type of clause to the doctrine – either because the doctrine does not apply or, more likely, because it is reasonable. Use or disclosure in defiance of such a clause is actionable as a breach of confidence or breach of an employee's duty of good faith. Similarly, the courts will not usually interfere with a type (c) covenant because breach is almost certainly a breach of the employee's duty of good faith (see *Hivac v Park Royal Scientific Instruments* (1946)), although it is possible they might interfere if the covenant effectively "sterilised" the employee's services (see Chapter 1).

The post-termination restrictions in (b) and (d) type covenants are clearly subject to the doctrine. A (b) covenant is also subject to a breach of confidence action if broken; and an interesting question is whether a valid restraint clause may go further in protecting confidential information post-termination than does the law on breach of confidence.

A (d) type of covenant is perhaps, of all the covenants, the one subjected to the most careful scrutiny; there are few cases where this type of covenant has been upheld. A further interesting comparison is between (b) and (d) types of covenant in terms of the courts' greater readiness to uphold the former and the type of information that they are prepared to concede justifies the covenant.

The nature of trade secrets has been considered in Chapter 1 in connection with actions for breach of confidence where there is no contractual restraint on use or disclosure. It may be, however, that the meaning of "trade secrets" widens to include certain other types of confidential information, at least when an express contractual restraint is involved.

The traditional meaning of "trade secret", so far as restraint clauses are concerned, can be seen in *Forster & Sons Ltd* v *Suggett* (1918). Here, the defendant had been employed by the plaintiff company in the business of manufacturing glass and glass bottles. He had acquired during his employment certain technical information concerning the manufacturing process and, in particular, the correct mixture of gas and air in the furnaces. The restriction in his contract which the plaintiffs sought to enforce prohibited him from being interested in or carrying on in the United Kingdom the business of glass bottle manufacture or any other glass-making business carried on by the plaintiff company. The court found no difficulty in upholding the restraint.

Note, however that this was a (d) type covenant, ie, the restraint in question did not specifically prohibit the employee from divulging or using trade secrets, but from working for a competitor in the business. It is therefore the mere *possibility* that the employee

41

might disclose or use trade secrets that is being protected. The employers do not need to prove use or disclosure, merely that the employee has that kind of information. This may have provided justification for the courts to take greater care in scrutinising the type of information the employee possesses as opposed to the situation where he has *actually* used or disclosed confidential information in breach of a duty of confidence or a confidentiality covenant. This is not necessarily the case, however.

In *Printers and Finishers Ltd* v *Holloway* (1964), the defendant, formerly employed as a manager in the plaintiff company, had *inter alia* copied some of the plaintiff's secret documents before taking up employment with a rival company. In this case there was no contract restraining him from doing so and the plaintiffs sought an injunction on general equitable principles. Although it was fairly clear that the defendant had acted in bad faith and had disclosed information to the rivals, as well as showing their representatives around his ex-employers' factory, the injunction was refused on the ground that none of the information in the defendant's possession amounted to a trade secret. Nevertheless, Cross J, in delivering judgment, tentatively suggested that the defendant's former employers might have protected themselves by an express covenant in restraint of trade. The reasoning behind this dictum appears to be that even an honest and scrupulous man may not realise he is passing on to new employers information regarded as confidential by his employer.

This, too, seemed to be the rationale of *Commercial Plastics* v *Vincent* (1964) where the defendant was employed as a research technologist in the plastics industry. He had agreed not to seek employment with any of the plaintiffs' competitors within one year of termination of his employment because of the "highly technical and confidential" nature of his employment. Although the clause failed for being geographically unlimited and therefore unreasonable, the court considered that the restriction would otherwise have been justified.

It seems therefore quite clear that so far as express covenants are concerned, no distinction is drawn between information which the ex-employee deliberately copies or takes away with him and that which he simply carries away in his head, possibly unaware of its confidential nature. The problem which the courts have set themselves is not to assess the degree of culpability of the defendant employee but to determine whether he had access to "trade secrets".

So far as breach of confidence is concerned, this also seems to be the case (*Faccenda Chicken* v *Fowler*), but deliberate copying or memorising may be caught by breach of fidelity (*Robb* v *Green*). Additionally, the fact that the information has been deliberately copied or memorised may give it the characteristic of being a "specific, separate body of knowledge" which in turn makes the possibility of its being deemed a "trade secret" more likely (see *Printers and Finishers Ltd* v *Holloway* and *Faccenda Chicken*).

It was pointed out by Lord Denning in *Littlewoods Organisation* v *Harris* (1977), which was a type (d) clause case (in which it is to be noted that the phrase "confidential information" was used in preference to "trade secret"), that the main problem is to distinguish what is highly confidential from what is not. In that case, the plaintiff employers ran a retail and mail order business and, together with their main rival, GUS, controlled two-thirds of all the mail order business in the United Kingdom. The defendant employee, who had been employed by the plaintiff company for more than ten years in their mail order business, latterly as an executive director, accepted an offer of employment from GUS. The plaintiffs sought enforcement of a restraint clause in his service agreement specifically prohibiting him from entering into a contract of service or similar agreement with GUS within twelve months of the determination of the agreement.

It was indisputable that the defendant had, during the course of his employment, acquired a great deal of knowledge about the conduct of the mail order business. The question was whether that knowledge was sufficient to amount to a trade secret. Caulfield J, at first instance, considered that it was not. He found as fact that the defendant knew virtually everything about the manner in which the plaintiffs ran their business, but concluded that there was nothing in the business that could properly be called a "trade secret".

The Court of Appeal, reversing his decision, disagreed. After quoting the above judgment and summarising the information which the defendant had in his possession, Lord Denning went on:

> "It seems to me that this bears the hallmark of confidential information. It has been acquired at great expense and by great expertise by Littlewoods."

It therefore followed that it ought not to be permissible for GUS to spare themselves equivalent trouble and expense by allowing a former employee of Littlewoods to take the information to them.

It seems quite clear from reading the judgments of the Court of

Appeal in this case that the original definition of "trade secret", which probably meant some kind of secret manufacturing process or formula, has been widened and now includes information which is so confidential that it is to be regarded as a "trade secret". The problem is that it brings us no closer to being able to identify what is and what is not confidential information amounting to a trade secret. Lord Denning's judgment acknowledges the difficulty, yet states categorically that the information in question "bears the hallmark of confidential information". What is this hallmark? Lord Denning merely refers to the expense and expertise required to obtain the information. It is submitted that this alone is hardly a reliable test of confidentiality and was surely not intended to be so. The other judgments go no further in identifying characteristics, merely stating that it would appear that the defendant possessed trade secrets or confidential information. The judges' opinions differ from that of the judge in the lower court, but none of them satisfactorily explains why. Browne LJ points out that Caulfield J appeared to have concluded that there were secrets but nothing so confidential as to justify a restrictive covenant; Megaw LJ appears to agree with counsel for the plaintiffs that it is quite sufficient to uphold the restriction if there is any confidential information equivalent to a trade secret. Yet it is not clear how he differs from Caulfield J.

On the other hand, it is clearly not every piece of confidential information which will justify a covenant. In *Morris* v *Saxelby*, Lord Atkinson described at length the charts, tables, drawings and other documents used by employers in the organisation of their business, including details of customer requirements, which he said were highly confidential but so detailed that an employee could not possibly carry them away in his head. He referred to this as a "scheme of organisation". The details were confidential but the employee's impressions of the scheme of organisation and business methods were not of a sufficient degree of confidentiality to warrant protection.

One of the main characteristics of the confidential information, as mentioned above, appears to be that it should be specific. In *Printers and Finishers Ltd* v *Holloway*, Cross J said:

> "If the information in question can fairly be regarded as a separate part of the employee's stock of knowledge which a man of ordinary honesty and intelligence would recognise to be the property of his old employer ..."

In *Faccenda Chicken* the Court of Appeal followed this judgment, refusing to hold that a "package" of information, in which none

44

of the items in itself amounted to a trade secret but the package as a whole was alleged to do so (it is not clear whether the court accepted this), could be protected. However, one explanation of *Littlewoods Organisation* v *Harris* might be that the court was prepared to accept such a package.

What other characteristics must the information have? In *Printers and Finishers* v *Holloway* (above), Cross J proposed as a test the understanding of an ordinary, honest and reasonable employee that the information would be the employer's property. However, in *Thomas Marshall (Exports)* v *Guinle* (see Chapter 1), Sir Robert Megarry VC bases his assessment of confidentiality on the *employer's* belief in the confidentiality of the information in the light of the usages and practice of the particular trade or industry. These two tests, although not wholly incompatible, might well come into conflict from time to time. In addition, it is submitted, neither an employer-based nor an employee-based test of itself guarantees the secrecy which is the principal ingredient of the information.

The problem is further complicated by the question of whether different standards are to be applied to different types of covenant, or where there is no covenant at all. The difficulty appears to stem from the dicta of Cross J in *Printers and Finishers* v *Holloway* where, in declining to grant an injunction against misuse of confidential information on equitable grounds, he indicated that the court might have been prepared to enforce a reasonable non-competition covenant. Neill LJ in *Faccenda Chicken* v *Fowler* rejected the first instance view of Goulding J that "category two" information (ie, information which the employee must treat as confidential during his employment but may use or disclose after termination) may be the subject of a restrictive covenant, on the grounds that *Morris* v *Saxelby* refers specifically to trade secrets. He then made a valiant, but not altogether convincing, attempt to reconcile this with *Printers and Finishers* v *Holloway* by identifying the type of information which he thought Cross J might have had in mind as being protectable by a restrictive covenant but not on general breach of confidence grounds. Possibly Neill LJ might have been implying that the "short-term trade secrets" he mentions (see Chapter 1) are not protected under equitable principles, but might be afforded protection by a reasonable covenant in restraint. Although one can see why a piece of information which is likely to remain confidential for only, say, one year might reasonably be protected by a restraint clause for one year, it is still a trade secret, and there is no reason why the court should not impose a one-year injunction under equitable principles. Indeed the information in *Littlewoods Organisation* v *Harris* appeared to be of that type, which may have been the source of Neill LJ's view, although he does not say so. If this reasoning is applied to the facts of *Printers and Finishers* v *Holloway*, it is hard to see that that was the type of information which Cross J had in mind. Dicta which seem to oppose Neill LJ's view concerning the protection of "category two" information under an express covenant can be found in *Balston Ltd* v *Headline Filters Ltd* (1987) (judgment of Scott J).

If there is such a thing as information which is not protected by the general law on fidelity or confidentiality but is protectable under an express post-termination covenant, then Goulding J's view would seem to provide the most sensible rationale of what it might be. Provided such information is carefully defined so that both parties understand what is included, there seems no reason why an employer should not be able to prevent at least actual use or disclosure, albeit for a limited duration, even though the information cannot exactly be called a "trade secret". It is submitted that the courts have been unwise in allowing themselves to be hamstrung by *Morris* v *Saxelby*. It was not the express view of any of the judges that *only* trade secrets (and no other confidential information whatsoever) might be protected by a restraint clause, and in any event, anything said about trade secrets was *obiter* in that case. Equally, with a doctrine based on public policy, public interest and reasonableness — which should be executed to develop to meet the changing needs of society — the courts are perfectly justified in departing from these dicta in the light of not only the tremendous developments in industry and technology since 1916 but also the many different kinds of confidential information which are now available. If the "trade secrets" category is not defined, it cannot be right to use it as a benchmark. The result is that too much time is wasted in court arguing what is or is not a "trade secret" and the judges are forced into the kind of vagueness demonstrated in *Littlewoods Organisation* v *Harris* when they feel there is information which deserves protection but which cannot be identified as a trade secret on any existing test.

It is, of course, arguable since *Faccenda Chicken* that Cross J's dictum no longer applies and that since "trade secrets" are protected with or without a covenant, and that the meaning is the same whether breach of confidence or restraint of trade is in question, it is not necessary to have a covenant in restraint at all. This is an unsafe proposition, however, since the courts continue to quote the dictum and try and reconcile it with *Morris v Saxelby*. So long as the law on breach of confidence remains separate from that on restraint of trade, and while the two grow so close as to provide a considerable overlap, the problem will remain: dicta in one case are obiter in the other and may be ignored. (See for example the discussion of *Systems Reliability Holdings* v *Smith* in the preceding chapter.) The court might be well advised to adopt the clearer breach of confidence guidelines in restraint cases.

If modern breach of confidence cases were to be seen as providing guidelines for restraint of trade involving confidential information, then Neill LJ's judgment in *Faccenda Chicken* does provide some very useful tests. Although it does not show exactly where to draw the line, it suggests that the following should be taken into consideration in deciding where to draw it:

(a) the nature of the employment – ie, whether an employee habitually handled material of a confidential nature so that he could be expected to realise its sensitive nature;

(b) the nature of the information – whether it is so highly confidential that it is equivalent to a trade secret;

(c) whether the employer impressed on the employee the confidentiality of the information.

If to these tests were added the tests of the employer's reasonable beliefs proposed in *Thomas Marshall (Exports)* v *Guinle*, it is submitted that the courts would find themselves with a very helpful set of guidelines on confidential information which may be protected under a restrictive covenant. The position would also be much clearer for both legal practitioners and for businessmen.

While the owner of the confidential information is protected by the breach of confidence rules, these will apply only where there is actual or intended use or disclosure of confidential information, which may be very difficult to prove and, in addition, will often assist the employer only when the damage has been done. If there is any justification for wide restraint by express clause, it is that the employee might inadvertently reveal the information without even stopping to think whether it is confidential. Although too great a restraint on the employee's liberty must be avoided, it is submitted that for the matter to be allowed to hang on proving that "trade secrets" have been imparted to the employee is too harsh to the employer; clearer tests would allow the employer properly to protect himself without endangering too much the liberty of his employees.

2. Customer connection

The other interest meriting protection for an employer (according to *Morris* v *Saxelby*) is his clientele. One can here see an analogy with business sale agreements for it may be almost as damaging for an employer if a key employee departs taking all the customers with him as it is for a purchaser whose vendor sets up in competition. However, there are distinctions. Firstly, in the case of a business sale agreement, the courts have been at pains to justify their favouring of the purchaser in terms of the monetary consideration he has paid for the goodwill (see Chapter 2). This argument cannot fairly be applied to employment contracts where the employer is paying for the work done, not for the employee's future loyalty. Secondly, in employment contracts, restraint clauses are often used not merely for anti-competitive purposes but to lock the employee into employment with an employer who has the freedom unilaterally to alter agreed terms and conditions or dispense with the employee's services at will (*Leather Cloth Co* v *Lorsont* (1869) per James J). Thirdly, there is the inequality of bargaining power mentioned above, where the employee is manifestly at a disadvantage. In the light of recent decisions concerning exclusive service contracts (*Clifford Davies Management Ltd* v *WEA Records Ltd* (1975) and *Schroeder Music Publishing Co* v *Macaulay* (1974)) one might expect this principle to be paramount in modern times. There is, however, no evidence that that is the case.

Here again there are a range of possible clauses for the employer's protection:

(a) a non-solicitation covenant to restrain the employee from soliciting customers for another business during his employment;

(b) an "exclusive services" clause, restraining the employee from working for anyone else (more usually a competitor) or otherwise competing with the employer during the employment;

(c) a post-termination non-solicitation covenant to protect the employer after the employment is terminated;

(d) a post-termination non-dealing covenant providing that the employee shall not deal or be concerned in the business of dealing in the same or similar products, goods or services as the employer;

(e) a post-termination non-competition covenant providing

that the employee is not to be involved in a business competing with the employer's after the employment is terminated.

"Exclusive services" clauses, as explained in Chapter 1, will usually be upheld so long as they do not "unilaterally fetter" the employee and "sterilise his services". In *Ehrman* v *Bartholomew* (1898), for example, an injunction was refused to a wine merchant in respect of his traveller who was employed under a ten-year contract to devote the whole of his time during usual business hours to the business of the wine merchant, and not to employ himself in any other business or transact any business with or for any other person, on the ground that it was too wide and should have been restricted to the same type of employment.

As to the other types of covenant, these are best considered under the separate headings of non-solicitation and non-competition.

(a) Non-solicitation covenants

Romer LJ said in *Gilford Motor Co Ltd* v *Horne* [1933] Ch 935 at page 966:

> "It is in my opinion established that when an employee is being offered employment which will probably result in his coming into contact with his employer's customers, or which will enable him to obtain knowledge of names of his employer's customers, then the covenant against solicitation is reasonably necessary for the protection of the employer."

This view has been criticised as being too wide because it is not every employee who has such a substantial contact with customers that those customers will be prepared to follow him. *Morris* v *Saxelby* included the additional ingredient of "influence" over customers which appears to narrow the field to those who ought reasonably to be restrained. Nevertheless, the wider view seems to have had a greater effect on the courts' thinking, at least in recent years.

In contrast to the position of a vendor of the goodwill of a business, a former employee, unless restrained by express covenant, is at liberty to canvass his former employer's customers (*Wessex Dairies Ltd* v *Smith* (1935)). However, to do so while still employed is a breach of his duty of good faith. As we have seen, an employee is also restrained by his duty of good faith from copying lists of customers (*Robb* v *Green*) or memorising them for the same purpose (*Coral Index Ltd* v *Regent Index Ltd*). The names of customers are not, however, confidential information amounting to a trade secret (*Baker* v *Gibbons* (1972); *Faccenda Chicken* v *Fowler*).

Non-solicitation covenants will be upheld more readily than non-competition covenants, because there is clearly a legitimate interest meriting protection, ie the employer's proprietary right in his goodwill (*Morris* v *Saxelby*), and because by their very nature they are reasonable as regards the extent of the business covered (*Lucas & Co Ltd* v *Mitchell* (1972)).

The matters which will attract scrutiny from the courts, therefore, are the extent of the business covered and the customers included under the covenant, and the duration (the latter being a matter of fact for the court to decide, taking into consideration all the circumstances of the case: see *Stenhouse Australia Ltd* v *Phillips* (1974) and *Dairy Crest Ltd* v *Pigott* (1989)).

It is also quite obvious that a covenant which restrains a former employee from soliciting does not prevent him working for or dealing with former customers of the employer who come to him out of their own accord, nor new customers who come to him on the recommendation of his former employer's customers (*Allied Dunbar (Frank Weisinger) Ltd* v *Frank Weisinger* (1988)).

The current approach to non-solicitation covenants may be seen from the decision of the Court of Appeal in *John Michael Design plc* v *Cooke* (1987). The defendants left their employment with the plaintiffs to set up a similar business of their own. Their contracts of employment had contained a covenant that they would not, for a period of two years from termination, canvass, solicit or accept from any client of the plaintiffs any business in competition with or similar to that of the plaintiffs. The plaintiffs sought an interlocutory injunction in respect of customers of theirs who intended to place business with the defendants and who, in any event, did not intend to place any further business with the plaintiffs. (NB: an interlocutory injunction very often decides the case in this situation because it prevents one party operating during the "make-or-break" period.) In the lower court it was decided that the balance of convenience favoured granting a general injunction but excluding the particular customer from its ambit − since the plaintiff would not get the business anyway. The Court of Appeal rejected this contention. The judges considered that there was no evidence to suggest the clause was invalid and granted an injunction covering all the plaintiff's customers, including the customer in question, on the ground that this was precisely the class of case against which the covenant was designed to give protection. The employer, it was said, does not need protection in relation to customers who are faithful to him. Although this seems correct in principle, it begs the question whether a customer who has decided not to do any further business with an employer can realistically be counted as part of the latter's goodwill.

As demonstrated in the *Weisinger* case, a non-solicitation covenant will not always, at least in the employer's view, go far enough to protect his clientele from a former employee's post-termination activities. He is therefore likely to want to impose a non-dealing and/or non-competition covenant, either instead of or, more usually, in addition to a non-solicitation covenant. The position where a non-solicitation covenant is deemed reasonable while a non-competition covenant goes too far is considered in Chapter 6.

(b) Non-competition covenants

There is an important distinction between non-solicitation covenants and non-competition (including non-dealing) covenants which ought not to be ignored when considering restraints in employment contracts. Solicitation involves a deliberate, possibly unethical, act on the part of a former employee. Merely working in a competing business, on the other hand, involves no deliberately immoral act and there is no guarantee that the employee will have, in his new employment, any contact whatsoever with his employer's customers. To uphold the latter type of covenant, therefore, is to prevent the employee earning his living in a particular way albeit that the employer might not be in any actual danger of losing business.

This raises the question of whether such a restraint on any employee's freedom to work is ever justifiable on the ground of customer connection. The situation is not parallel to the trade secrets situation: there is clear justification for non-disclosure of trade secrets – industry would collapse if trade secrets could be freely disclosed, and we have a whole body of law dedicated to confidentiality. A non-competition covenant founded on trade secrets, it is submitted, is justifiable because a former employee might reveal a trade secret "inadvertently" while working for a former employer, perhaps simply by allowing people to watch him work. It is difficult to restrain this type of potentially serious disclosure, especially given the vagueness which surrounds the concept of a "trade secret".

On the other hand, a covenant based on customer connection has traditionally been justified with reference to his goodwill which is his "most saleable asset", a justification which was still being used by Harman LJ in 1970 in *Home Counties Dairies* v *Skilton*. Yet this goodwill is not protected by the general law in the absence of a covenant. Even in relation to the goodwill attaching to the sale of a business, the courts have found it necessary to seek additional justification in terms of the consideration paid for the goodwill. Any idea that the employer is giving consideration to an employee in return for the goodwill which that employee generates has long been abandoned and there are, as explained earlier in this section, other reasons which favour the disallowance of this sort of covenant.

With *Morris* v *Saxelby* (supported by other earlier cases) on the one hand, and the kind of considerations outlined above on the other, it is hardly surprising if non-competition covenants in employment contracts have caused more problems to the court than any other express restraint. In one of the earlier cases, *Mason* v *Provident Clothing and Supply Company Limited* (1913), the appellant was employed as a canvasser for the respondent clothing and supply company who carried on business on "the check and credit system" in London and Middlesex. The employment agreement provided that the appellant would not for three years after termination be employed in or engage in any business similar to the respondents' within twenty-five miles of London. It is notable that, the respondents having failed to argue any specific ground on which the covenant might be justified, the House of Lords paid scant attention to the goodwill which the employee might have generated (which would seem to have formed the obvious ground for the covenant); their lordships were more concerned with whether the appellant possessed any trade secrets. What little they did say about the goodwill, however, is illuminating: Lord Shaw was of the opinion that a reasonable non-solicitation covenant would have been enforced. "Reasonable", it is implied, meant confined to the area in which the appellant actually canvassed. The actual covenant, Lord Shaw said, attempted to deprive the appellant of his freedom to dispose of his labour or to advance himself. Viscount Haldane thought that a covenant not to canvass in the area where he had actually assisted in building up the goodwill might have been upheld. He also expressed the view that the appellant's abilities were mainly due to his natural gifts as a canvasser and in a secondary degree to special training. The clause was struck down as being too wide.

Over the decades following *Mason*, rules emerged which led to the generally held view that it was necessary to subject employer-employee covenants to more rigorous tests than any others. The courts showed a strong reluctance to enforce non-competition covenants, except where there was a very strong personal connection between an employee and a customer, such as doctor-patient or solicitor-client relationships, or where there was special familiarity with the customer's requirements and repeated dealings, such as between insurance brokers or stock-brokers and their clients. In addition, the covenant, in order to be struck down, had to be so limited that it was effectively a non-solicitation covenant. Where there were in the contract both a non-solicitation covenant and a non-competition covenant, the courts were inclined to uphold the former at the expense of the latter.

It is against this background that the reasoning in recent Court of Appeal cases requires careful examination. In *Marion White Ltd v Francis* (1972) the defendant employee was a ladies' hairdresser employed in the plaintiffs' salon. The restraint covenant in her contract of employment was long and complex and included a non-solicitation covenant and prohibitions on being engaged, concerned or interested in, in any capacity, the business of a ladies' hairdresser, attending clients in their own homes, letting her name be used in connection with any ladies' hairdressing business and inducing any of the plaintiffs' clients to leave them. The geographical area was half a mile and the duration of the restrictions was twelve months from termination. The defendant's employment contract ran for a fixed term of twelve months but she was dismissed (justifiably, as it happened) before the end of the term. The covenant was upheld.

There are several interesting features. By the time the case reached the Court of Appeal the twelve months restriction had expired and the court was making a purely declaratory judgment. The Court of Appeal therefore had no reason to consider the balance of convenience nor involve itself with equitable principles. A declaration as to the reasonableness or otherwise of the covenant as it stood was all that was required. The agreement was of relatively short duration and, it can be argued, customer connection made during that period could not have been very strong. There appeared to be no evidence to suggest that the defendant was so skilled at her job that clients would wish to retain her services – indeed the fact that she was dismissed before the expiry of the fixed term might suggest the opposite. Nor was there any indication that clients did actually follow her when she took employment with a nearby rival.

Given the fact that the defendant had negotiated the clause, and in view of the relatively short duration and small area, it is not suggested that the decision was incorrect in terms of reasonableness. However, in view of the above factors, one might question whether the employer should have received any protection at all and, even if he was entitled to protection, surely a non-solicitation or non-dealing covenant would have sufficed – and a covenant which prohibited the defendant from being in any way involved in ladies' hairdressing in any capacity was too wide.

The court did not think so. In addressing the contention that the covenant would have prevented the defendant from being employed as a receptionist in a hairdressing salon, Buckley LJ remarked:

> "If that is what he [the High Court judge who had held the covenant to be too wide] had in his mind, I would myself think that that would be likely to be just as damaging or almost as damaging to the goodwill of the employers as employment in the actual processes of attending to hair ... "

Why? Because the plaintiffs' customers would still be likely to follow her. It does not say much for the quality of the plaintiffs' business if their customers are likely to go to an untried salon merely because the receptionist had once styled their hair. It says even less for their customers who apparently cared so little for the service they were receiving. This view, with respect to the Court of Appeal, is as naive in its assessment of modern consumer demand as it is insulting to the intelligence of women who are customers of hairdressing salons.

A similarly patronising approach to the consumer was noted above in connection with the *Frank Weisinger* case and one can see the same attitude being given expression in the earlier case of *Home Counties Dairies Ltd* v *Skilton* (cited in *Marion White* v *Francis*) where, after waxing lyrical about the "familiar figure" of the milkman of his youth, Harman J described the modern milkman as:

> "... a familiar and probably influential character well known to every householder in the road. It is natural in the circumstances that he acquires, usually on behalf of a master, a clientele along his round who, if he is an agreeable and competent man will tend to rely on him for his arrival and to follow his departure to serve another employer."

With the modern tendency being to deliver milk early in the morning, it is perhaps questionable whether most people even know their milk roundsman and it is certainly an extremely doubtful proposition that (in the absence of active solicitation) customers would, instead of simply accepting deliveries from the dairyman's replacement milkman, actively seek out their old milkman with his new employers and place their business with them. (Added to which to suggest that a milkman is "influential" is surely stretching a dubious argument to its limits.)

The actual restraint clause with which the court was concerned in *Skilton* was a combined non-solicitation and non-dealing clause which, rather than prohibiting employment with a rival (albeit that that might be the practical effect) restrained the employee from canvassing, soliciting or being concerned in the supply of milk and dairy produce to customers of the old employer. Argument centred mainly around the width or otherwise of the words "concerned in the supply of ... dairy produce", which it was alleged might have prevented the defendant from being employed in a shop or restaurant which sold cheese. This was at least in part a non-solicitation covenant (there was evidence to the effect that Mr Skilton, who had taken employment with a competitor, had in fact solicited some of his former employer's customers) but, if the Court of Appeal considered that to be a relevant fact, it did not say so. Nor did it say anything to suggest that it was applying different principles than it might have done had it been a non-competition covenant. Indeed, had the Court of Appeal done so, the decision could not have been so easily followed in *Marion White* v *Francis*.

After many decades of the courts refusing to uphold covenants where the customer connection was not strong, what are we to make of these cases where certainly the nature and duration of the employment involved do not suggest that the customers would be strongly tied to the employees? Let us return for a moment to consider the public interest requirement – which has somehow come to be subsumed in the parties' interests but, although neglected, still hovers like a wraith over the whole question of restraints. In some of the old cases, restraints in the public interest were justified by reference to the theory that an employer would not employ people to work for him if he could not restrain them from taking his trade secrets or his customers to a rival. The public interest, it was said, was secured by allowing the employer the widest possible choice of labour (see *Mallan* v *May* (1843) 11 M & W 653 and the judgment of Parke B at page 666). This is not (and probably never was) wholly true, since employers do not act out of philanthropic motives but employ, for their own benefit, the best people they can get. It is unrealistic to suggest that, in the absence of the right to use reasonable restraints, they would employ only persons so useless or dim-witted that there would be no danger of losing them to a rival. In reality, they would employ the best people they could, take the risk and do everything possible to keep them. If the public interest *is* in the widest pool of labour being available, then it is best served by not tying employees to one employer.

However, defining public interest in those terms may have been in accordance with the prevailing economic view that capital was paramount above labour. Later, the view emerged that employers had a "proprietary right" in the goodwill of the business while the public interest lay in not depriving the public of the employee's services by removing him from the labour pool for long periods. It was in order to balance these two interests that the courts developed the "protection no greater than reasonably necessary" principle.

Where does that leave us today, when a century has completely changed the face of commerce? Unfortunately, it seems that many judges are relying on the same old justifications and definitions of the public interest that were current in their youth. In modern times, when the consumer is king, and even the legal profession is expected to operate according to market forces, one surely expects the public interest to lie with former employees being free to compete with as little restriction as possible. In addition to which, since the vast majority of the general public are now employed in some position or another, public interest might be said to be more properly identifiable with that of the employee.

Fairness, of course, decrees that the employer be robbed of nothing of value belonging to him. The point has, however, already been made that it hardly accords with modern economic thinking to regard a customer as a mindless chattel belonging to the employer, against whose irrational behaviour the employer deserves protection. Leaving aside the exceptional kind of businesses such as solicitors and medical practices where it is in the nature of things that the customer will form a strong attachment to the person who attends him rather than to the practice as a whole, it is submitted that there are two kinds of goodwill. First, there is the goodwill engendered by the firm itself. It may comprise clean and attractive premises, a policy of treating the customer with promptness, courtesy and efficiency, an attractive corporate image, an excellent complaints procedure and any number of other things of this nature.

Second, there is the goodwill engendered by a particular employee, because of his own personal skills, talents and personality rather than anything the employer has taught him. It is submitted that, rather than being a mindless chattel, the modern consumer is very well able to distinguish between the two and to make his own decision, according to perfectly rational good sense, whether to remain with the company or follow the employee. The kind of judgment, for example in *John Michael Design plc* v *Cooke*, which interferes with his liberty to make that decision, can surely not be in the modern public interest.

It is further submitted that goodwill engendered in the former way ought properly to be deemed to belong to the employer, while that gained through the latter is really the employee's own, since the employer does not pay for it. To take an extreme case, suppose that the employing business is a bad example of its kind. Suppose however that there is one employee who is so skilled that customers come to rely on him and recommend their friends to him. If the employee, tired perhaps of bad working conditions and lack of support from his employers, leaves to set up his own business or to work elsewhere, is it realistic to say that the goodwill engendered by him belongs to the employers who have paid nothing over and above what they have paid other employees who are not so skilled and have brought them nothing?

However, that appears to be the justification in the above cases for the shift back towards favouring the employer.

That is not the whole story. It is not hard to discover a common feature in those cases which is shared with the even more difficult case of *Littlewoods Organisation* v *Harris* and with a third case which may be included here, the facts of which are as follows.

In *Lucas & Co Ltd* v *Mitchell* (1972) the defendant was a salesman employed by the plaintiffs. The restraints in his contract of employment comprised two elements: (a) dealing in certain goods in the Greater Manchester area, and (b) soliciting the former employer's customers in that area. There was proven solicitation of some of the customers, but the covenant as it stood was too wide because it prevented the defendant from dealing with potential customers with whom he had had no previous connection. The Court of Appeal found that it could split the covenant into the two distinct elements and apply the doctrine of severance so as to uphold the non-solicitation covenant while striking out the other.

Clearly the court was influenced here by the fact that the defendant *had* solicited his former employer's customers. In *Marion White* v *Francis* , Buckley LJ said that the conduct of the defendant had been ethically quite inexcusable.

In *Skilton* the same moral viewpoint is clear. Cross LJ expressed the view that a covenant should not be deemed void as contrary to public policy where the former employee had been in flagrant breach of it.

In *Littlewoods Organisation* v *Harris*, Lord Denning, in criticising the judgment in *Commercial Plastics Ltd* v *Vincent*, said he thought the court should have upheld the covenant in restraint of trade because the defendant had tried to break both the wording and the spirit of it.

Even in *John Michael Design plc* v *Cooke*, where there was no discussion of reasonableness, an argument advanced by the plaintiff's counsel to the effect that the court ought not to support the situation where a party, aware of a non-solicitation etc clause, deliberately promotes a breach of it, was regarded by O'Connor J as worth taking into consideration as having "some validity", although it was not of any very great importance.

In all the other cases, the covenant was too wide. In each case its ambit was restricted by the court – in *Lucas* v *Mitchell* by severance, and in the other two cases by reading in limiting words. The means will be discussed in Chapter 6. The point is that the Court of Appeal seems to have found a new strength to uphold covenants which it would not have upheld thirty or forty years ago. It seems that, if the employee has behaved "unethically" and has done that which a narrower interpretation of the covenant would have prevented, then the court will tailor the covenant so as, effectively, to punish him. The new trend may stem from equity or from moral indignation and may be a wholly justifiable interpretation of the doctrine, but it is certainly not applying the restraint doctrine as seen in *Morris* v *Saxelby* and *Mason* v *Provident Clothing and Supply Co Ltd*.

The time-honoured approach is to look at the contract at the day it was made, in relation to circumstances then existing, and decide whether the clause is wider than necessary to protect the legitimate interests of the employer. The new approach, apparently, is to look at what the employee has done and ask whether it was within the contemplation of the parties when the agreement was made. If it was, then it is fair that he should be restrained. This casts doubt on the long-held principle that a restraint is valid or void *ab initio*.

The new approach may have been influenced by the House of Lords' approach in the *Clifford Davies* and *Schroeder Music Publishing Co* v *Macaulay* cases and may mark a new era in which a test of fairness is to be substituted for that of reasonableness, albeit with opposite effects in the two types of case. If so, the court has not said so but has relied on older lines of authority to justify its view.

3. Financial incentives

Although a contract of employment is not usually analogous to a business sale agreement in this respect, it may be that an employer will offer some additional consideration in return for an employee's agreement to accept a restraint clause.

The consideration may be taken into account by the court when weighing the reasonableness or otherwise of the restraint, but it is not the court's task to determine the sufficiency of the consideration (*Hitchcock* v *Coker* (1837)). It is deemed sufficient if it has more than illusory value (*Austen* v *Boys* (1858)). Nor will the court perform a weighing exercise to decide whether the probable benefits accruing to the covenantor or the detriment to the covenantee under the covenant are proportionate to the consideration received (*Allied Dunbar* v *Frank Weisinger*).

A straight payment for taking a restrictive covenant is likely to be offered only to key employees. Such payments have in the past been used as a way of giving such employees extra remuneration free of income tax, but the legislature has enacted provisions to close this loophole. Section 313 Income and Corporation Taxes Act 1988 provides that:

> "(1) Where an individual who holds, has held or is about to hold an office or employment enters into an undertaking (whether absolute or qualified, and whether legally valid or not) the tenor or effect of which is to restrict him as to his conduct or activities ..."

any sum paid by way of consideration for the undertaking is treated as an emolument subject to Schedule E income tax. Sums paid include (a) sums paid in respect of the giving of the undertaking, or its total or partial fulfilment, either to the individual giving the undertaking or to any other person, and (b) sums which do not otherwise fall to be treated as an emolument.

Payments under a contract of employment were taxable under the Income and Corporation Taxes Act 1970, but payments under separate agreements would not be taxable but for s 313 of the 1988 Act.

Only the higher rate of tax is payable on agreements entered into before 9 June 1988. On or after that date, both higher and basic rates are payable. However, such a payment is deductible as trading expenditure for the employer, and is a management expense for an investment company (s 73 Finance Act 1988).

In *Vaughan-Neil* v *IRC* (1979) it was held that a payment to a barrister to induce him to cease practice and to take up employment was not caught because it did not include undertaking the very duties which are inseparable from the employment itself, and thus was not in respect of a relevant undertaking.

Other forms of consideration than payments of monetary sums may be given, and it is not unusual for employers to extract restraint covenants in return for paying a pension, for example, as the following cases demonstrate.

Wyatt v *Kreglinger and Fernau* (1933): The plaintiff retired from the defendant's employment, and the defendant wrote offering him a pension. The letter said: "You are at liberty to undertake any other employment or enter into any business, except in the wool trade, and the only other stipulation we attach to the continuance of this pension is that you do nothing at any time to our detriment (fair business competition excepted)."

The Court of Appeal held that this was a contract in restraint of trade; since it was unlimited in time or space, the Court of Appeal considered it to be unenforceable. However, the plaintiff was deemed to be not entitled to the pension because there was no other consideration for it than the willingness to accept the restraint. This case may be contrasted with *Bull* v *Pitney-Bowes Ltd*.

Bull v *Pitney-Bowes Ltd* (1966): The defendants were manufacturers of franking machines. The plaintiff was an employee and it was a condition of his employment that he must become a member of the company's non-contributory pension scheme. A rule of this scheme stipulated that if a retired member engaged in any activity or occupation which was in competition with or detrimental to the interests of the defendants, he was liable to forfeit his pension rights. The plaintiff retired and took up employment with a similar business. He was threatened with the loss of his pension and sought a declaration that the stipulation was void as being in restraint of trade.

Here, the reasoning in *Wyatt* v *Kreglinger and Fernau* was followed and the rule was held to be void. However, as the pension scheme was not consideration for the restraint (or vice versa), the plaintiff was entitled to his pension.

In *Sadler* v *Imperial Life Assurance Co of Canada Ltd* (1988) the financial incentive was to be found in the contract of employment itself. The plaintiff was an insurance agent with the defendants and his contract of employment provided for him to be paid commission in respect of premiums paid during the first ten years of a policy he had sold. This meant, of course, that there would be commission payable after his employment had been terminated. This was provided for in the contract, which stated that an agent's entitlement to such commission would cease if the agent entered into a contract of service or for services "directly or indirectly with any limited company, mutual society, partnership or brokerage operation involved in the selling of insurance". The plaintiff did in fact breach this clause.

In holding that the clause was unenforceable as being in restraint of trade, the High Court considered that there was no distinction between this and the situation in *Wyatt* v *Kreglinger and Fernau* and *Bull* v *Pitney-Bowes*: the plaintiff was being offered a financial incentive to accept an unreasonable restraint clause and the clause was void. The court also held that the invalidity of the restraint did not make the obligation to pay post-termination commission avoidable on the ground of failure of consideration.

The cases thus make it clear that the courts are not prepared to entertain the argument that an additional financial incentive is sufficient to validate a restraint taken by an employee, nor to regard that restraint any more favourably than in any other case.

4. Shareholders' agreements

Shareholders' agreements sometimes contain restrictive covenants, and where an employee holds shares in his employer company, it is not beyond the bounds of possibility that an employer might try to impose restrictions in a shareholders' agreement or share sale agreement to which he is subject. The question is whether such restrictions will be treated in the same way as restrictions in pension agreements and in respect of pension payments as above, or whether they are more properly restrictions in connection with the transfer of the goodwill of a business. As we saw in Chapter 2, the court has upheld a covenant against an employee which was contained in a share sale agreement, despite the fact that the commercial reality appeared to be that the intention was to restrain him in his capacity as an employee rather than as a vendor.

WAC Ltd v *Whillock* (1990), a Scottish case, concerned another situation which is becoming increasingly common. There was a management buyout by the plaintiff company in which the defendant and others were director-shareholders. A shareholders' agreement between them and the company contained a non-competition clause for the period that they were shareholders and for two years after their ceasing to be so. Although the Court of Session made no attempt to categorise the agreement, it interpreted its provisions very strictly so as to hold that the defendant had not breached the covenant and, in doing so, relied on the authority of employer-employee cases.

5. Restraints in third party agreements

In *Kores Manufacturing Co Ltd* v *Kolok Manufacturing Co Ltd* (1958) two rival competitors in the field of products involving secret chemical processes agreed by an exchange of letters that neither of them would at any time employ any person who had been an employee of the other within the preceding five years. It was held by the Court of Appeal that this agreement was in restraint of trade and was unreasonable in the interests of the parties. This is perhaps a surprising decision in the light of what has gone before, since there was clearly some confidential information to be protected and the effect, if upheld, would have been to deny the employee employment with only one company. However, the court's view was that this was the same as a covenant in a contract of employment and, relying on *Morris* v *Saxelby* the court applied rigorous principles in deciding whether there were trade secrets to be protected.

6. Names

It may be that the employee has engendered a great deal of goodwill for his former employers by the use of his own name or a pseudonym which has become famous: actors, models and television personalities, for example. Fairly obviously, the employers cannot restrain a former employee from working for anyone else under his own name, but where a pseudonym is used which has been invented for the employer's purpose, is there a better case for saying that any goodwill which it generates belongs to the employer so that he can restrain its use by the employee? Apparently not. In *Hepworth Manufacturing Co Ltd* v *Ryott* (1920) the plaintiff film producers employed the defendant as an actor. As required by his contract, he acted under a particular pseudonym which was said to be the property of the plaintiffs, and after termination he was prohibited from using it for any purpose whatsoever. Moreover, the contract provided that he could not work for anyone else unless they agreed not to use the pseudonym in announcing or advertising his performance. These prohibitions were held to be in restraint of trade and unenforceable, as they went further than necessary for the employer's protection. An important factor in the case was apparently that the defendant's "market worth" would be diminished by more than 50 per cent if he could not use the pseudonym. However, whether such a restriction is to be upheld or not seems to depend very much on the circumstances and, in particular, on the nature of the employment.

7. Conclusions

A few brief conclusions may be drawn by way of providing some guidelines:

- Restrictions are placed on the employee's external activities during his employment by his duties of fidelity and confidence.

- Those duties extend after termination of his employment only to the extent that they prevent him using or disclosing trade secrets belonging to his former employer.

- Express contractual restraints on an employee's activities during his employment will be upheld so long as they do not "sterilise his services".

- Express contractual restraints on his activities after his employment has terminated will be upheld only if there is a genuine danger that the employer's trade secrets will be disclosed or his goodwill affected.

- To be upheld, the restraint must not be too wide in its scope; the courts may cut down or interpret a wide restraint and are especially liable to do this where the employee has acted in breach of the spirit of the restriction.

- Restraints sought to be imposed on an employee otherwise than in his contract of employment are likely not to be upheld if they are taken as consideration for a pension, or if they are contained in a third party agreement, but may be upheld if they are contained in a share sale agreement.

Chapter 4

Directors' service contracts and partnership agreements

Partners and executive directors are not the same as others working within the business to be protected because they will (usually) be closely involved in the management of the company. This close involvement will mean that at least some of them will have close contact with, for example, customers and suppliers of the business. Additionally, if the business has any trade secrets or confidential information amounting to a trade secret, it is more likely than not to be known to the directors or partners. The courts have therefore, over the years, shown themselves more ready to accept that the company or partnership has a legitimate interest meriting protection against post-termination activities.

At the same time, with the norm being for executive directors to hold qualifying shares in the company, both partners and directors are in most instances owners of a proportion of the goodwill of the business. Where shares in the partnership or business are sold on termination or retirement, it is easier for the courts to apply the vendor-purchaser rules rather than the strict employer-employee rules, especially where the rules are contained in a sale or shareholders' agreement.

Finally, a proposed director or partner will often be in a far stronger bargaining position than the rank-and-file employee. He will to some extent be in a position to negotiate terms which he considers to be reasonable. He will, in the case of a partner, and may, in the case of a director, receive consideration for accepting restraints on his future employment: a share of the goodwill for a partner, and perhaps shares or a monetary payment or pension arrangements for a director. On the takeover of a company's

64

business or in connection with a management buy-out, directors may enter into non-competition covenants to preserve the goodwill.

All these considerations mean that a court will more readily uphold as being reasonable a restraint taken from a director or partner. Nevertheless, while the court may be more inclined to concede that there is an interest meriting protection, and may be more lenient in considering the precise limits of the clause, it will still strike down anything which appears to it much wider than is necessary for the employer's protection.

As mentioned in Chapter 1, the general law itself provides a number of restraints on the activities of directors and partners, and it is necessary to consider these alongside the court's attitude to restraint clauses.

1. Directors' service agreements

In *Gilford Motor Co Ltd* v *Horne* (1933), a managing director of a company entered into a service agreement with the plaintiff company which contained a non-solicitation covenant by him personally. After leaving the plaintiff company's service, he formed a company of his own which solicited the plaintiff company's customers. The court took a very hard line indeed (already noted in the last chapter) and held that the company was a sham to cloak his wrongdoing.

Remarks made in that case about employer-employee non-solicitation covenants have, as noted above, been criticised but it is probable that the case demonstrates a harsher attitude towards directors as a sub-class within the category of employees. The fact that the defendant had been a director in the plaintiff company may go some way towards explaining the court's attitude in both *John Michael Design plc* v *Cooke* and *Littlewoods Organisation* v *Harris* (see Chapter 3).

Despite the fact that it is seemingly easier to enforce a contract in restraint against a former director than against other types of employee, the modern trend appears to be towards restraining directors through their implied duties rather than by express ties in their contracts of employment.

Executive directors owe their company duties (in addition to duties of care and skill) of good faith as an employee and as a director and of confidentiality. The extent of these duties has come under scrutiny in a number of cases.

Bell v *Lever Bros Ltd* (1932): B and S were employed by L Ltd under contracts of service as chairman and vice-chairman of its wholly owned subsidiary N Ltd. B and S began speculating in cocoa in competition with N Ltd so that L Ltd, had it known, would have been justified in terminating their service agreements. On a later merger, L Ltd, still in ignorance of the speculation, paid B and S compensation in respect of termination of their service agreements. Later, L Ltd discovered the truth and sued for return of the compensation payments. It was held *inter alia* that B and S were under no implied duty to disclose their speculative activities, although there was competition with the company, nor (in the absence of any express restraint) was there any duty on a director not to set himself up in competition with his company. (NB: a director who competes may nevertheless be in breach of his duty of fidelity as an *employee* (see *Balston Ltd* v *Headline Filters Ltd* below) or of an exclusive services clause in his contract (see Chapter 3).)

Island Export Finance Ltd v *Umunna* (1986): The defendant was the plaintiffs' managing director. He secured a contract for the plaintiff company with a certain organisation. Subsequently, he resigned from his position with the company and set up a company of his own which obtained orders from the same organisation. It was held that the defendant was not in breach of his duty of good faith to the plaintiffs.

In *Bell* the rationale was that the directors' speculative transactions, although concerned with a commodity in which the company was interested, were in no way concerned with any contract in which the company itself was concerned. Similarly, in *Umunna*, the exploitation of the business was not his primary objective in leaving the company; nor, when he subsequently obtained business from the organisation, were the plaintiffs actively pursuing that business. It could not be said to be a "maturing business opportunity" belonging to the plaintiff. This case may be contrasted with *Industrial Development Consultants Ltd* v *Cooley* (1972) (full facts in Chapter 1), where the director, who resigned in order to take on his own account business which he had been negotiating on behalf of the company, was held to be in breach.

Quite clearly, where the director takes for himself the benefit of a contract belonging to the company, he will be held to account. In *Cook* v *Deeks* (1916), Company A had four directors who were also shareholders. Three of the directors who, between them, held the majority of shares, were negotiating a lucrative contract for the company. Instead of making Company A a party to the contract, however, they formed Company B, a company wholly owned by them, and took the contract in the name of Company B. It was held that the fourth shareholder in Company A could sue them and recover the benefit of the contract for Company A since there had been fraud and misappropriation of company property.

Cook v *Deeks*, of course, was based on the fact that the contract was really Company A's property, but in *Industrial Development Consultants Ltd* v *Cooley* the company could not have obtained the contract and so the cases are distinguishable on that basis. Nevertheless, there is a common feature in the lack of *bona fides* shown by the directors. If it is lack of good faith which underpins the reasoning in this area then we still have to reconcile the case of *Regal (Hastings) Ltd* v *Gulliver* (1942). In *Regal (Hastings) Ltd*, the defendant and others were directors of the plaintiff company which wished to take a lease of two cinemas. The lessor refused to grant the lease because the company was under-capitalised, and the defendants therefore formed and raised finance for a subsidiary company which was granted the leases of the cinemas. The venture was profitable and the defendants were eventually able to sell out their shares in the subsidiary for a profit. It was held that the defendants must account to the company (now under new ownership) for their profit on the shares, although they had acted in good faith throughout, had used their own money – not the company's – to buy the shares, and the company itself could not have obtained the benefit of the leases.

Perhaps, as has been suggested by some company law commentators, the explanation is that there is a wide range of fiduciary duties owed by a director, with *Cook* v *Deeks* at one end, *Regal (Hastings) Ltd* v *Gulliver* at the other and *Industrial Development Consultants Ltd* v *Cooley* somewhere in the middle.

In Canada, a different approach has been taken (*Peso Silver Mines Ltd* v *Cropper* (1966)). However, it is not easy to say whether the Canadian court disagreed with *Regal (Hastings) Ltd* v *Gulliver* or whether it was merely establishing a boundary to directors' liability. The plaintiff company was offered an opportunity to acquire certain claims which, after careful consideration, it rejected. Three of the company's directors then formed a syndicate to acquire the claims for themselves. The court held that they were not obliged to account to the plaintiff company for profits made out of the claims. The distinction between this and the *Regal* case, or indeed the *Cooley* case, may be that the contract remains a corporate opportunity, albeit one that the company may not at the time be able to obtain, until the board acting properly and in good faith rejects it. However, it is arguable that if this is the case it may encourage the directors to be less than totally committed in pursuing the opportunity on behalf of the company or considering whether the company should accept or reject it.

The position seems to be that a director is not prevented from working or being concerned in a business competing with that of the company while he is still a director, so long as his contract does not contain an "exclusive services" clause (the rules concerning which can be seen in Chapter 3) but it will be a breach of his duties of good faith if he takes a profit from any contract obtained through his position as a director, unless the company has expressly rejected that contract. So far as the continuance of the fiduciary duties after termination is concerned, these would appear to continue only in so far as the defendant did not begin his breach, like *Cooley* while he was still a director.

So far as confidentiality is concerned, a director will be bound by the same rules as everyone else. *Balston Ltd* v *Headline Filters Ltd* (1990) has reviewed the whole law relating to a director's implied duties of confidentiality and of good faith as an employee and as a director. In that case, the plaintiffs were manufacturers of filter tubes. Each grade of tube was manufactured to a particular recipe and the plaintiffs claimed that the recipes were trade secrets. H was an employee and director and gave notice to terminate his employment, with a termination date of 11 July 1986 which allowed him to exercise a share option on 9 July. He bought an "off-the-shelf" company (the defendant company, H Ltd) and agreed to take a lease on certain business premises (although he alleged that he had not decided to set up in business when he gave in his notice). In May, a customer of the plaintiffs, C Ltd, telephoned H and told him that the plaintiffs had increased their prices and were prepared to supply C Ltd for only a limited period. On 8 May, H visited C Ltd and it was agreed that the latter would place an order for filter tubes with the defendant company for delivery from 14 July. From then on, H admitted to making active preparations for H Ltd to commence manufacturing the tubes. This included hiring employees, including some employees and ex-employees of the plaintiff company, and buying equipment.

There were restraint clauses in H's contract of service with the plaintiffs but it was agreed by the parties that these were too wide and the plaintiffs proceeded on the basis of breach of fiduciary duty, breach of an employee's duty of good faith and misuse of confidential information.

It was held on the first count that so long as there was no active competition while H remained a director, and he was not diverting a "maturing business opportunity" to himself, there could be no breach of fiduciary duty. He was, however, in breach of his duty of good faith as an employee when he came into active competition for the business of C Ltd in May and he had also breached his duty by approaching an employee of the plaintiffs, and offering her employment with H Ltd. On the question of confidential information, it was held that the recipes were in fact confidential information, but since H had the skill and expertise to produce recipes of his own it could not be held that he had misused the confidential information belonging to his former employers.

Thomas Marshall (Exports) Ltd v *Guinle* (1978) (referred to in Chapter 1) also concerned a director. The defendant was managing director of the plaintiff company. His service agreement stipulated:

(a) that he was not to engage in any other business without the company's consent while he was employed as managing director;

(b) that during and after his employment, he was not to disclose confidential information in relation to the affairs, customers or trade secrets of the company and its group;

(c) that after ceasing to be managing director, he was neither to use nor disclose confidential information about the suppliers and customers of the group, nor for a period of five years employ any person who had worked for the company during the last two years of his appointment.

While still managing director, the defendant traded on his own account and, through two companies owned by him, with the plaintiffs' customers and suppliers. He also employed some of the plaintiffs' former employees. He resigned as managing director and the plaintiffs applied for injunctions to restrain the defendant from soliciting orders from the plaintiffs' customers, dealing with their suppliers and disclosing or using confidential information or trade secrets belonging to the plaintiffs.

It was held that the defendant was in breach of both his fiduciary duties as a director and his obligation of fidelity as an employee. It was also held that the use of the confidential information for his own purposes was a breach of his duty of fidelity. The injunctions were granted as requested. It is interesting to note that, although the wording of the restrictions was discussed and clearly considered relevant, the question of unreasonable restraint of trade does not appear to have been raised, the defendant merely contending that the agreement having come to an end, he was no longer bound by its restrictions. However, it is doubtful whether the court would have held that the restrictions were void as sterilising the director's services (see Chapter 1).

If the courts take a strict line in interpreting restraint clauses, especially, as has been seen, in the area of trade secrets, it is reasonable to expect employers to attempt instead to push back the barriers of good faith, especially where it appears that the director has been at fault.

However, the outcome of *Balston Ltd* v *Headline Filters Ltd* is a lesson to those who would rely on the implied duties, and the clear message for the practitioner is to draft in express covenants wherever possible.

2. Partnership agreements

The case of a partnership agreement is analogous to neither a contract of employment nor a business sale agreement. The courts have therefore declined to be bound by the guidelines for either category and have treated the case of a partner as something separate (see Lord Fraser in *Bridge* v *Deacons* (1984)). The extensive duty of good faith owed by partners to one another has already been mentioned in Chapter 1, where it can be seen that partners owe duties of good faith to one another in excess of fiduciary duties of directors, because of the requirements to reveal to the other partners everything relevant to the partnership business and not to compete. It has not usually been argued, however, that these duties extend to cover a partner after retirement or dissolution. As a partner is an owner rather than an employee, he will not owe an employee's duty of fidelity. It is therefore usual to bind partners by post-termination restrictions in the partnership agreement. Such restrictions will be valid provided they satisfy the usual requirements (*Whitehill* v *Bradford* (1952)). There may of course also be restraint clauses which cover the period of partnership and so make the position as to what is restricted as clear as possible, and again these may be upheld (*Morris* v *Colman* (1812)). Despite the fact that the agreement falls neither into one category nor the other, absence of post-dissolution restraints will mean that a partner can behave as the vendor of a business without restraints, ie he can set up in competition anywhere, deal with former customers and advertise his connection with the old business (*Churton* v *Douglas* (1859); *McFarlane* v *Kent* (1965)), but he may not solicit the old customers or use the old name or otherwise imply that he is carrying on the old business (*Boorne* v *Wicker* (1927); *Curl Bros Ltd* v *Webster* (1904)).

In the field of confidential information, the rules do not differ substantially from those applicable to employees. One characteristic difficulty arises, however. Confidential information, like other property of the partnership, is owned in common. As part owner, does a partner, in the absence of express restrictions, have the right to use or divulge that information after retirement or dissolution? Although one can argue that on retirement the information ceases to be his property and becomes that of the continuing partners, this question has not, so far as can be ascertained, been discussed, and it is clearly wise to make some provision in the partnership agreement.

So far as solicitation is concerned, a partner, being more closely concerned with the management of a business than a shareholder, is likely to be involved with clients. Indeed, in professional partnerships, most business is obtained through a partner's personal connections. It is, of course, arguable that if a partner has brought the customer into the business, he should be entitled to take that customer with him when he leaves. However, it may be that a client brought in by one partner is "serviced" by another and develops a stronger connection with that other. The position then is less clear.

There are two types of partnership where the partners involved will have a strong connection with customers: medical practitioners and solicitors. In both such cases, post-termination restraints are advisable; if carefully drawn, they are likely to be upheld.

(a) Medical practitioners

The medical practitioner is in a peculiar position because he is both a partner in the practice and an employee of the National Health Service. He is therefore already restricted in the sense that he will usually be obtaining employment within the National Health Service. Two points have been raised in connection with this: first that a covenant not to practise might be illegal by virtue of s 35 National Health Service Act 1946. Secondly, that in a National Health Service practice there can be no goodwill for the clause to protect. The judges have fought rather shy of deciding either point. As regards the former, Stamp J in *McFarlane* v *Kent* (1965) held the clause in question to be valid subject to anything in s 35 which would make it illegal; and they are likely to be valid if they impose no wider restraint than is reasonably required (*Whitehill* v *Bradford* (1952); *Kerr* v *Morris* (1986)). As regards the second point, he said ([1965] 2 All ER 376 at page 381):

> "I felt some doubt whether a covenant not to practise at all within a prescribed area, being designed to protect the goodwill of a medical practice, which cannot be sold and which has no significant number of paying patients, could ever be reasonable."

Although it was not necessary to decide the point, since the claim on the basis of that particular express covenant had been abandoned, it was his *obiter* opinion that a non-solicitation covenant would have been quite enough to protect the goodwill since all the patients were known by name.

In *Peyton* v *Mindham* (1971) Plowman J also refused to decide the point since the covenant was unenforceable on other grounds.

A point which has been the subject of much judicial discussion, as can be seen from both *Peyton* v *Mindham* and *Lyne-Pirkis* v *Jones* (1969), is whether the covenant may be invalidated because it could prevent a medical practitioner from operating as a consultant.

Lyne-Pirkis v *Jones* (1969): A general medical practitioner in Godalming was restricted by a clause which stipulated that for five years from his expulsion or retirement from the practice he was prohibited from engaging in practice as a medical practitioner either alone or jointly with any other person within a radius of ten miles from Market House, Godalming. It was held that the words "medical practitioner" could include "consultant".

This case was followed in *Peyton* v *Mindham* (1972) where the restriction on the partner was "not to professionally advise, attend, prescribe for or treat" any person who had been a patient of the partnership. In reliance upon dicta of Lord Greene in *Routh* v *Jones* (which had concerned a medical assistant rather than a partner) to the effect that a consultant's practice could hardly injure a medical practitioner's practice, it was held that the covenant was too wide. It is, however, interesting to note the difference between this approach and that taken in *Home Counties Dairies Ltd* v *Skilton* (see Chapter 2) which suggests that the robust approach taken to employment contracts in recent times has not been extended (surprisingly, since they have always been taken to have more in common with vendor-purchaser agreements) to partnership agreements.

(b) Solicitors

That solicitors and their clerks have a special relationship with their clients, which not only gives them a strong customer connection but often knowledge of very intimate and personal details relating to clients, has long been recognised. This brings a particular danger for the business when an outgoing partner or ex-employee sets up in competition or goes to work for a competitor. For this reason even a general anti-competitive covenant is likely to be upheld if reasonable. In *Fitch* v *Dewes* (1921), a solicitor employed at Tamworth an articled clerk who subsequently became his managing clerk. His contract of service provided that, if he left the solicitor's employment, he would never practise as a solicitor within seven miles of Tamworth Town Hall. This covenant was upheld, despite its life-long duration, because the clerk had become well acquainted with the details of the solicitor's clients. (NB: it has been suggested that such a restraint would probably be held void nowadays.)

A modern point of importance is the position of "associate solicitor" or "salaried partner". In *Briggs* v *Oates* (1990), the defendant was an assistant solicitor with the plaintiff and the plaintiff's partners, having been the plaintiff's articled clerk. He was given the status of associate solicitor and, two years later, was appointed to the position of "salaried partner" under an agreement which provided that he would not "either during the continuance of the agreement or during the five years after its determination, practise as a solicitor within a radius of five miles" from the plaintiff's office nor solicit any of the clients of the firm who were clients "either prior to or during the partnership". It can be argued that the clause was too wide anyway, but the point at issue was, since the partnership had been dissolved, could the defendant still be bound by the restrictions in the agreement. Scott J considered that on a true construction of the agreement (the defendant was to be paid by salary and a commission, take no share in the profits, and be responsible for no losses) the agreement was a contract of employment which was brought to an end by the dissolution of a partnership (as to the termination of agreements containing restrictions generally, see Chapter 10).

Perhaps the most important case on solicitor partnerships is *Bridge* v *Deacons* (1984), a Privy Council case which sets out a number of guidelines for construing restraints in such agreements. Here the respondent firm was one of the oldest and largest firms of solicitors in Hong Kong. The appellant was employed by the firm; and some years later he became a full partner. The partnership agreement provided that no partner ceasing to be a partner should for five years thereafter act as solicitor in the Colony of Hong Kong for any person, firm or company who was at the time of his ceasing to be a partner or had during the period of three years prior thereto been a client of the partnership. The practice was subsequently departmentalised and the appellant, who was in charge of the intellectual and industrial property department, had no contact with 90 per cent of the firm's clients. In 1982, he retired, transferring his share of the assets to the continuing partners, and set up his own firm.

Several interesting guidelines appear from the judgment:

(a) the court decided that the legitimate interest was not restricted to those clients for whom the appellant had acted;

(b) the court stated that partners are the owners of the whole assets, including the goodwill, and the whole goodwill may be protected so long as protection does not extend beyond the practice;

(c) the court considered that mutuality was an important consideration in relation to partnership contracts. The clause in question restricted all partners equally and was therefore fair. On the other hand, a clause which prevented an outgoing partner from acting only for those clients for whom he had previously acted could operate unfairly as between partners with a large number of clients and those with very few or none;

(d) the Privy Council expressed disagreement with dicta of Lord Denning in *Oswald Hickson Collier & Co* v *Carter-Ruck* (1984) where a similar restraint clause was considered to be contrary to public policy because a client ought to be able to choose his solicitor. The Privy Council thought this was not of general application;

(e) the court also considered that the fact that the partners were experienced solicitors argued that they thought the restrictions reasonable, and some weight should be attached to this view:

> "... some weight should be given to the fact that the restriction is found in a partnership agreement which has evidently been carefully drafted and which must be taken to represent the views of experienced solicitors who would be well aware that an unduly severe restriction would be unenforceable."

3. Conclusions

Directors' service contracts and partnership agreements are each in some way special. Although the courts have been reluctant to categorise partnership agreements and seem to regard them as falling into a category wholly of their own, directors' service agreements are usually treated as normal employment contracts. Nevertheless there are indications that restrictions in directors' service agreements are regarded more leniently than those in other contracts of employment. In construing partnership agreements, on the other hand, the court is more often influenced by the principles applicable to the sale of the goodwill of a business. The following points may be noted by way of summary:

- Directors are subject to wide duties of good faith during the continuance of their employment as directors.

- These duties will not normally extend beyond termination unless the director has betrayed a trade secret or embarked on an act of bad faith or was in breach of a fiduciary duty during his employment which continues after his employment has been terminated; some express provision is therefore necessary to cover the situation.

- Express contractual restraints are treated to the strict tests applicable to restraints in any employment contract, but it will often be easier for the employer to prove there is an interest meriting protection in respect of a director than in respect of other employees.

- Partners are subject to considerable restraints as part of their duty of good faith while they remain partners; nevertheless it may be worth clarifying some of these in the partnership agreement.

- After retirement or dissolution, the duty of good faith is no longer owed, although there may be a duty of confidentiality; in the absence of express restraint, partners may do as they wish so long as they do not solicit old customers or purport to be the old firm.

- Express restraints are more likely to be construed according to the less rigid principles applicable to the sale of a business, but the principle of mutuality appears to be paramount.

Chapter 5

Tying agreements

In this category are included agency, distribution, "solus" and franchising agreements. These agreements share some similar restrictions. In particular, the covenantor will often be "tied" to a particular brand of goods or services by an exclusive purchasing clause and/or an exclusive selling clause, and restrictions will flow from the need to restrict competition with others authorised to deal in products or services of the same brand.

The court is perhaps more inclined to uphold sole agencies and exclusive distributorships than other types of "exclusivity" agreement. In *Esso Petroleum Co Ltd* v *Harper's Garage (Stourport) Ltd* (1967) Lord Pearce said that sole agencies were a "normal and necessary incident of commerce" and indicated that the court would uphold restrictions aimed at maintaining the exclusivity provided that any restriction on taking on work other than under the contract absorbed the services of the agent, rather than sterilised them.

However, the general thrust of the judgments in *Esso* is that all agreements are potentially within the scope of the doctrine (and, as we have seen, restrictions during the existence of the contract may also be subjected to the test of reasonableness), so a better view of Lord Pearce's judgment is perhaps that a sole agency or distributorship is not *of itself* invalid so long as it does not go beyond what is necessary or usual to protect the exclusivity of the agency. It is, however, likely to be subjected to scrutiny and found invalid if one party is so unilaterally fettered that the contract restricts competition rather than promotes trade. The fact that sole agencies and distributorships have rarely come before the courts may be due to their having taken on a standard form through long usage. It is also the fact that, in more recent times, restrictions which are usually to be found in these agreements have come to be controlled through restrictive practices legislation.

"Solus" and franchising agreements are agreements which go further than containing exclusive purchasing and/or exclusive selling clauses. Here, the covenantor's relationship with the covenantee is highly integrated and the covenantee can expect to control, through restrictions, such matters as the hours when shops are to be kept open, the way in which the shops are fitted out, and what other products are to be sold. Nevertheless, as they are essentially more complex types of distribution arrangement, one expects broadly the same principles to apply to them as apply in any other form of agreement.

Ties in respect of any distribution arrangement may be caught by Article 85 of the Treaty of Rome and this aspect is considered in the next chapter.

1. Sole agency

In English law, an agent is someone who does acts for and on behalf of another (the principal). The concept is very wide indeed and it is certainly not every agency which will be caught by anti-competitive rules. In this section, we are concerned mainly with agencies forming part of a manufacturer's distribution network.

A businessman will often use the words "agent" and "distributor" interchangeably in this situation, but for legal purposes they have quite different meanings. English law regards the agent, while acting within the scope of the agency, to be a vital organ of the principal — his right arm, so to speak. The contracts which he makes for the principal will be the principal's contracts and torts which he commits may render his principal liable. Similarly, EEC law regards true sales agents as no more than an arm of the business they represent, so that Article 85 does not apply to the agreements appointing them. However, it also recognises another category, the commercial agent who is defined as a self-employed intermediary who has continuing authority to negotiate the sale or the purchase of goods on behalf of the principal, or to negotiate and conclude such transactions on behalf of and in the name of that principal. The United Kingdom differs from other member states of the EEC in that it does not have a specific body of law for the regulation of agreements between commercial agents and their principals. However, the Directive of 18 December 1986

"On the coordination of the laws of the member states relating to self-employed commercial agents" requires changes in the law relating to commercial agents by 1 January 1994.

For the present, agency agreements and any restrictions in them are dealt with under the common law and the law relating to restrictive practices and resale price maintenance (where applicable). Sole (or exclusive) agency is quite common and, so far as the doctrine in restraint of trade is concerned, the courts will uphold a restriction in an agency agreement which prevents the agent from acting for anyone else during the currency of the agreement (see Lord Hodson in *Esso Petroleum* v *Harper's Garage*). The court will also uphold restrictions aimed at preventing an agent from disclosing confidential information belonging to the principal, or using it for his own benefit, but such restrictions are unnecessary during the course of the agreement since the agent has wide fiduciary duties – at least commensurate with an employee's duty of good faith, and possibly wider.

So far as post-termination restrictions are concerned, the principal must have an interest meriting protection. The interest may be trade secrets in which case the usual rules will apply. So far as customer connection is concerned, the agent's customers are his principals. The customers with whom he transacts business on behalf of his principals are his principal's customers and part of the principal's goodwill. There is, of course, a possibility that an agent may set up in competition with his principal at some later stage. In deciding how best to construe any post-termination restrictions in this kind of agreement, the court is likely to avoid categorising it and instead to consider the substance rather than the form of the agreement and examine the surrounding circumstances in order to decide what is most reasonable in the particular situation. (See, for example, *Sadler* v *Imperial Life Assurance Co of Canada Ltd* (1988); *Office Overload* v *Gunn* (1976).)

2. Distributors

A distributor is usually a retailer who buys goods from a manufacturer and re-sells them. Provisions in the agreement vary but there will usually be an exclusive purchasing clause by which he must purchase all the products he sells from the manufacturer or other authorised persons and an exclusive selling clause by which he is given a particular sales area ("territory") in which he has the sole right to sell the manufacturer's products.

A selective distribution system is one where the manufacturer selects a number of "approved dealers" who are the sole distributors he is prepared to supply with his products and then imposes restrictions preventing them from reselling to anyone except end users and other approved dealers.

Parallel trading is a form of dealing whereby a trader buys goods in one area and sells at a higher price in another. He will usually operate outside the manufacturer's distribution network; since the practice of parallel trading has a tendency to force down prices, manufacturers are concerned to impose restrictions aimed at preventing the practice. These will usually be in the form of preventing approved dealers from selling outside their territory as well as imposing restrictions on the use of trade marks and, in extreme cases, forming price-fixing cartels.

A wide range of anti-competitive practices is therefore possible in the context of a distributorship agreement. In so far as these have come before the courts under the restraint of trade doctrine, the court recognises the benefits for the general public in allowing manufacturers to impose restrictions so that they may operate an efficient distribution network (see the judgments in *Esso Petroleum* v *Harper's Garage* and *Petrofina* v *Martin*). Nevertheless, the court will not uphold restrictions which go further than is necessary to protect the distribution system in question. Nor will the court be prepared to uphold any naked anti-competitive covenants which are ancillary to the subject-matter of the agreement, for example accessory products of the manufacturer or supplier. (See further solus agreements below.)

Any provisions in a distributorship agreement which amount to restrictive trade practices or resale price maintenance will of course render the agreement subject to the legislation and it will have to be registered and its restrictions may be examined by the Restrictive Practices Court. Since most restrictions which manufacturers wish to impose on their distributors fall within this category, they have come to be considered by the Restrictive Practices Court rather than under the restraint of trade doctrine.

EEC law also recognises the benefits to be had by the consumer or end user from a good distribution system and is accordingly also more lenient with restrictions in distributorship agreements, exempting them from the provisions of Article 85 provided that they conform to certain requirements. Restrictions which are unusual, and especially restrictions aimed against parallel trading and those which would enforce a price-fixing arrangement, are dealt with particularly severely (see Chapter 7).

3. Solus agreements

A solus agreement is in essence an exclusive purchasing agreement, differing from other distributorship agreements in that it is usually collateral to a transaction in which the main purpose is the sale oɪ lease of land and premises or the provision of mortgage finance. The covenantor agrees to buy all the products he sells from the covenantee, who is also usually the seller, lessor or mortgagor of the premises. Typically, he will also enter into other covenants imposing restrictions on the way in which the business is run, and possibly requiring him to sell other products. The petrol companies "invented" the solus agreement to establish a distribution system by tying in purchasers of petrol stations to their brand of petrol, but a similar familiar type of arrangement has been in existence for over a century whereby breweries tie public houses to their brand of beer, restrictions usually being ancillary to the grant of a lease on the relevant public house.

The solus clauses may be contained in a separate agreement or in the main document (conveyance, lease, mortgage) itself. There is often a provision that the owner of the premises can sell them only if he ensures that the purchaser takes over the solus obligations. The agreement to be enforced may not then be that between the original parties.

Solus agreements have received more attention from the courts under the restraint doctrine than other agency or distributorship agreements and the cases provide some useful general guidelines.

As was explained in Chapter 1, the solus agreement case of *Esso Petroleum Co Ltd* v *Harper's Garage (Stourport) Ltd* (1967) is an important landmark in the history of the restraint doctrine, containing much of the modern law in connection with restraints as laid down by the House of Lords. It will be recalled that in both that case and in the earlier Court of Appeal case, *Petrofina (Great Britain) Ltd* v *Martin* (1966), the respondents had agreed to buy their petrol exclusively from the appellants. There were also other clauses concerning resale price maintenance and the times at which the garages should be kept open. While in both cases the House of Lords and the Court of Appeal were unanimous in their decision as to the validity or otherwise of these agreements, the basis of their decisions varies.

Looking first at the *Esso* case, the later of the two, there were two agreements. The first, relating to Garage M, bound the respondents to buy petrol from the appellants at their prevailing wholesale prices for four years and five months. The second, relating to

Garage C, was identical and bound them for twenty-one years. The judges in the House of Lords were unanimous in their opinion that the agreements were subject to the doctrine. They held that the agreement in relation to Garage M was reasonable since five years was not in the circumstances longer than was necessary to afford adequate protection to the legitimate interests of the appellants which lay in maintaining a stable distribution system. However, the second agreement was held to be void. The basis of this view was that twenty-one years went beyond any period of reasonably foreseeable development which would affect the distribution network, and there was no evidence to the effect that a shorter period would not have been adequate.

Lord Reid explained that the legitimate interests of the covenantee in this type of agreement must necessarily depend largely upon the state of affairs in their business, which must be considered in relation to the distribution and sale of petrol generally. These, he said, were questions of fact to be answered by evidence or common knowledge. He considered that there were advantages to both parties in such agreements. In relation to the appellant's claim that five years was not unreasonable, he appeared to consider it most relevant that the appellants could organise their business better if only one-fifth of their ties on average came to an end in any particular year and he rejected as impracticable the test proposed in the Court of Appeal: a test which would have meant establishing whether the appellants could have found other suitable outlets in the area within two or three years. With regard to the second agreement, it was argued for the appellants that, as the respondents had used the appellants' money to build up the business, it would be unfair to the appellants if the respondents were to be free after a fairly short period to seek better terms on which to purchase petrol from a competitor. Lord Reid did not accept this argument. He said that he did not have any material on which to assess its weight and was not therefore in a position to determine its validity. The main factor which influenced him here was that the producing company, Esso, could not show a greater advantage to either themselves or the garage owners in the longer tie.

Lord Hodson accepted that the tying covenant in the agreement was necessary for the protection of continuity of outlets for the company's petrol in the area in which the garages were situated. He found the five-year period reasonable, largely because five years had been considered a reasonable period in earlier Commonwealth cases and had never been stated to be unreasonable in English cases. (This case and, to some extent, the *Petrofina* case, are rare in that the duration was considered to be the determining factor.) In deciding that the twenty-one year tie was unreasonable, Lord Hodson stressed that he was basing his decision on the public interest. He considered this to be a surer foundation than the interest of private persons or corporations when widespread commercial activities of that nature were concerned. He also put forward a criterion for judging the reasonableness or otherwise of a clause in restraint of trade. This criterion originated in a judgment of Lord Greene MR and is to the effect that the fundamental basis for reforming mortgage transactions is to strike down an unconscionable bargain. This, Lord Hodson, considered, should apply equally to contracts in restraint of trade.

It is interesting to note in passing that this dictum is echoed in the later exclusive services cases. It is also interesting to note the reliance on precedent to assess reasonable periods of duration, which approach was rejected by the Court of Appeal (without the judgment in *Esso* being cited) in *Dairy Crest Ltd* v *Pigott*).

Lord Pearce based his decision on commercial efficacy. He appeared to believe that the system of tying agreements had resulted in improved and more efficient distribution of petrol. He, too, relied on other cases, notably Canadian and South African, in which a five-year period had been held to be reasonable in relation to tying agreements, and expressed the opinion that if the court were to hold five-year periods to be too long, it would be out of accord with modern commercial needs, would cause embarrassment to the trade and would not safeguard any public or private interest which, in his view, needed protection. He would not have regarded the twenty-one year period as unreasonable had there been a right of the respondent to terminate it before that time (the "unilaterally fettering" criterion noted in Chapter 1). He was also influenced by the fact that the tie did not add anything to the protection of the security since the supplier had a discretion not to supply if his own sources of supply were to fail him.

Lord Wilberforce, again in reliance on the periods specified in previous cases, decided that a period of five years was not unreasonable but that twenty-one years was too long. Like Lord Hodson, he was at great pains to point out that, although the case had been fought on the question of reasonableness as between the parties, the public interest should not be forgotten. Unlike Lord Hodson, however, he did not base his decision on the public interest.

Turning to consider *Petrofina* v *Martin* by way of comparison, the facts were that the respondent had signed a solus agreement as a condition of his agreement to purchase a garage from the original covenantor under the agreement. The solus agreement was to continue for twelve years during which the respondent undertook to buy all his petrol from the appellants, to use only their lubricating oil, to advertise only their lubricating oil, to keep the garage open at all reasonable times and not to part with the garage unless the third party agreed to observe all the conditions of the solus agreement.

Lord Denning thought that if public houses could be tied, there should be no reason why this liberality should not apply to petrol stations too. In fact, he considered that to be the best argument in favour of solus agreements. In his view, the early solus agreements might have been held unreasonable because the large companies were probably merely concerned to obtain protection from competition *per se* but there was justification for a comparatively small company like the plaintiffs' protecting its interests under a solus agreement since it could so easily be "swallowed up by its giant rivals".

Nevertheless, Lord Denning was not prepared to accept the argument that the covenant was reasonable merely because it was restricted to only one facet of the business. He regarded it as unreasonable on the ground of duration because there was no escape for the owner of the garage, whatever difficulties he might have to face, although there was an escape clause for the appellants. Given this factor, a twelve-year tie was unreasonable, although a two-year tie might have been reasonable. He also considered that the provisions concerning the lubricating oil were naked anti-competitive covenants and were void. Finally, he considered as unreasonable the tying of a third party to the solus agreement, because it meant that if the respondent could not get a buyer on those terms he might have to continue running the garage at a loss solely for the benefit of the appellants.

Harman LJ, in the minority, argued that the appellants did not have a legitimate interest to protect, an argument which is no longer tenable since *Esso Petroleum* v *Harper's Garage.*

Diplock LJ appeared to be in agreement with Lord Denning both as to his view that there was a legitimate interest to protect (although he was clearly not happy with this view and referred to solus agreements as creating "a new commercial serfdom"), and as to the unreasonableness of the duration. He was more forcibly in agreement with Lord Denning's judgment on the latter point and was greatly influenced by the fact that, however great the respondent's losses, he could not give up the business for twelve years. Diplock LJ declined to express any opinion on how long might have been considered reasonable by the court.

In *Alec Lobb (Garages) Ltd* v *Total Oil (Great Britain) Ltd* (1985), the Court of Appeal surprised the legal profession somewhat by upholding as reasonable a covenant in a solus agreement for twenty-one years, clearly looking to the particular circumstances of the case rather than regarding *Esso Petroleum* v *Harper's Garage* as having created a duration precedent for solus agreements. The facts were that the garage was in financial difficulties and re-negotiated its solus agreement with the supplier. The new agreement provided that for a premium of £35,000 the garage would be leased to the suppliers for fifty-one years at a peppercorn rent and then leased back to the shareholders in the garage for twenty-one years. The garage company sought to have the agreement set aside on the ground *inter alia* that it was in unreasonable restraint of trade.

The defendant was unable to prove that the ties in the agreement were necessary, but in holding that the agreement was reasonable, the Court of Appeal was influenced by the following factors:

    (a) the benefit of £35,000 accruing to the garage company;

    (b) the site could be used only as a garage and it made little difference to the public whether the petrol sold on it came from that company or another;

    (c) the garage company could terminate the tie after seven years;

    (d) the premises had already been tied for four years before the new tie was agreed;

    (e) (*per* Dunn and Waller LJJ) if the court were to uphold the agreement, it would encourage the rescue of other firms in similar financial difficulties.

Some useful general guidelines may be drawn from these cases concerning tying agreements:

- the fact that restrictions are contained in some other agreement, eg a mortgage, does not mean they cannot be subject to the restraint doctrine;

- whether or not there is an "escape route" for the covenantor may be of paramount importance in determining whether restrictions are reasonable or not;

- ties in this sort of agreement are justifiable if the effect is to provide an efficient distribution network which would otherwise not be possible;

- ties of up to five years are likely to be upheld, provided that the tie is generally justifiable on the above ground, on the basis that they have previously been upheld, but they ought not to go beyond what is absolutely necessary;

- ties for over five years become less and less justifiable as the duration increases, but a long-term tie can be justified if there are special circumstances which warrant it and if there are provisions making it especially reasonable, such as additional consideration paid to the covenantor or an "escape route" for the covenantor;

- there is some doubt whether the court considers the parties' interests, the public interest, or both, but the current approach in the Court of Appeal, at least, seems to be to look at the agreement as a whole to determine whether in the circumstances the restrictions were unconscionable.

As mentioned above, Lord Denning was greatly influenced in his view that the petrol companies had a legitimate interest to protect by the fact that breweries had been tying their tenants under exclusive purchasing agreements unchallenged since the last century. The brewery agreements seem to form a separate class which are excluded from the ambit of the doctrine. In *Esso Petroleum* v *Harper's Garage* it was suggested that the form and terms of these agreements had been hallowed by negotiation over long years so that they enjoyed universal commercial acceptance (see Chapter 1). It has also been suggested that the reason is because they are contained in the agreement under which the public house is acquired, although this is perhaps a weaker argument, given the dicta of the House of Lords in *Esso Petroleum* v *Harper's Garage* to the effect that the type of agreement in which the restrictions are contained does not usually affect the case.

Exclusive selling and purchasing clauses which may be subject to the doctrine are not restricted to petrol and beer, however. In *Servais Bouchard* v *Prince's Hall Restaurant Ltd* (1904), for example, an agreement by which the proprietor of a restaurant agreed to buy all his burgundy from a particular seller was held to be in unreasonable restraint of trade. Equally, an exclusive selling agreement, whereby a producer agrees to sell all his product to a society or association, is subject to the doctrine. Instances of this latter type of agreement are provided by *McEllistrim* v *Ballymacelligott Co-operative Agricultural and Dairy Society*

(1919) (milk) and *English Hop Growers Ltd* v *Dering* (1928) (hops). In the first of these cases, the producer was prevented from trading in a wide area and there was no provision by which he could determine the agreement. This was held to be an "unusual and excessive fetter on the farmer's personal liberty". In the second case, the agreement had been accepted by the great majority of hop producers and moreover contained nothing unusual, and accordingly it was upheld.

4. Franchising

The International Franchise Association defines "franchising" as:

> "a continuing relationship in which the franchisor provides a licensed privilege to do business, plus assistance in organizing, training, merchandising and management in return for consideration from a franchisee."

In EEC law, it is defined as:

> "a package of industrial or intellectual property rights relating to trademarks, trade names, shop signs, etc., to be exploited for the resale of goods or the provision of services to end users and which includes at least:
> - the use of a common name or sign and a uniform presentation of contract premises and/or means of transport
> - the communication by the franchisor to the franchisee of secret substantial marketing and sales know-how, capable of conferring a competitive advantage on the latter
> - the continuing provision by the franchisor to the franchisee of commercial or technical assistance during the life of the agreement."

The word has not been defined in English law.

The three main types of franchise are the product franchise, the trade name franchise and the business format franchise. With the first two, the franchisees concentrate on one company's product line and to some extent identify their business with that company. With these, the simplest form of arrangement is the agency or distribution agreement mentioned above or what we know as a simple licensing agreement, and not what in England is regarded as a franchise proper. Examples exist in the motor and soft drinks industries. The third type is the one we are more likely to think of as a franchise, hamburger chains such as McDonald's being a prime example. Here the relationship between the franchisor and franchisee is fully integrated. The franchisee is selling, under the franchisor's trade mark or brand name, a standardised product or products from standardised premises. Staff will often wear a standard uniform and there may even be standardised procedures. All these standardisation features will be obtained by restrictions under the franchising agreement, which will also contain restrictions aimed at protecting any know-how passed to the franchisee by the franchisor and the goodwill in the particular territory in which the franchisee operates.

Although franchising in this form has been around for a very long time in the United States and Canada, it is a comparatively recent import to this country. There are a number of distinct advantages to the franchisee in a franchise arrangement. First, he gets to use a brand name and trade mark made popular by the franchisor, which gives him a distinct advantage in the market over those who have to start up "cold" with a product of their own. The franchisor will have done most of the groundwork in building up the goodwill for the brand name before the franchisee comes on the scene. Secondly, the franchisee is likely to benefit from wider advertising and promotions sponsored by the franchisor. Thirdly, the standardisation controls mean that the customer knows more or less what to expect and may thereby be encouraged to patronise the franchisee rather than take a risk with an unknown quantity. Fourthly, some of the larger franchisors offer a wide range of additional benefits such as training, financial assistance and counselling. We therefore expect the courts to regard the franchise agreement as not wholly bad and one in which the restraints are justifiable by the need for strict standardisation controls aimed at maintaining the franchisor's reputation for quality and by a perfectly legitimate interest in preserving the know-how passed on to the franchisee, protecting the use of any patent, trade mark or brand name, and protecting the territory of other franchisees.

The English courts have had little opportunity of considering franchising agreements in the context of the restraint doctrine. The Canadian courts have, however, subjected the territorial restrictions in franchising agreements to the restraint doctrine and have cut down a restriction prohibiting a franchisee from competing in any other area where he could have been granted a franchise as well as his authorised territory, but have upheld a clause restraining a franchisee from competing in the same area as his franchise (see *Big Iron Drilling Ltd* v *Standard Holdings Ltd* (1981)).

The English court had to consider a franchise agreement in *Prontaprint plc* v *London Litho Ltd* (1987) which concerned post-termination restrictions rather than those during the currency of the agreement. The plaintiff company operated a printing franchise. The defendant was a former franchisee who continued the business after expiry of the franchise agreement at the same premises but under a new name. The plaintiffs sought to restrain him from doing so on the basis of the following restriction contained in clause 17 of the franchising agreement:

> "the licensee agrees that he shall not at any time within three years of the determination of this agreement engage in or be concerned or interested directly or indirectly in the provision of the Service or anything similar thereto within a radius of ½ a mile of the premises or within a radius of 3 miles from any premises in the United Kingdom at which the Service or anything similar thereto is carried on by any other licensee or by the licensor itself",

and a non-solicitation covenant which provided that:

> "the licensee shall not for two years thereafter knowingly solicit or entice or attempt to solicit or entice away from the licensor or any of its other licensees persons who at the date of termination or within the preceding two years were customers or employees of the licensor or any of its other licensees".

The defendant argued that the clause was unreasonably wide and that during the subsistence of the agreement payments made to the plaintiffs were in respect of the use of the trade mark and know-how and other assistance, and therefore the goodwill belonged to the defendant who had built it up and was not the plaintiff company's to protect. The court disagreed. It considered that the agreement, although different from a business sale agreement, was closer to that than it was to an employer-employee agreement, and held that the plaintiff company did have a legitimate interest in the goodwill because the defendant had achieved his business success by using their trademark. The payments made were not purely in consideration of the know-how and goodwill, but were also made in consideration of a protected interest under a franchise.

So far as the restraint doctrine is concerned, then, the franchise agreement will be subject to the liberal interpretation reserved for business sale agreements; there could be few restrictions wider than those in the Prontaprint agreement, given that any member of the public in any area might have used some aspect of the Prontaprint service at some time or another, and it would have been virtually impossible for the franchisee to determine who these people were. The restrictions therefore effectively removed the franchisee from the whole business of printing or anything similar for two to three years following the expiry of the agreement. This may be contrasted with the approach in the Canadian courts, who seem perhaps to regard it as closer to the employer-employee situation.

If control of restrictions in franchising agreements under English law is minimal, some agreements are nevertheless subject to control under EEC law, where territorial restrictions at least have been held to have an anti-competitive effect. (See further Chapter 7.)

Those who draft franchising, solus and distribution agreements will usually have a great deal of experience in this field, and it is not possible to consider in detail the wide range of clauses which may be included in these agreements. Since they are hybrid agreements, many of them will be subject to rules or guidelines mentioned in other parts of the book. For those advising potential franchisees or other types of licensee, a short section has been included in Chapter 9 on what to look out for generally in these kinds of agreement.

5. Licensing

Patent, trade mark and know-how licensing agreements are all a matter for the expert and well outside the scope of a modest work such as this. However, many agreements, including the above, may contain a provision or two the aim of which is to protect this sort of intellectual property, and it is of some use to have an idea how the court will regard such restrictions. The protection of confidential information gleaned from employment or sold as part of a business sale has been dealt with in the relevant chapters. However, how will the court proceed when it is a matter of a limited licence to use the information?

A limited licence might include some or all of the following restrictions:

- the licensor is restrained from competing with the licensee in respect of the same or similar products or services within a particular area or from licensing others to do so;
- the licensee is restrained from using or disclosing the information otherwise than within the strict limits of the licence;

- the licensee is restrained from competing with other licensees in other areas;
- restrictions on either party on dealing in competing products or services.

So far as the restraint doctrine is concerned, the court is likely to consider the agreement as more akin to a business sale agreement: the parties are on equal footing; consideration is given; there is an interest meriting protection. See, for example, the Canadian case of *Tank Lining Corporation* v *Dunlop Industrial Ltd* (1982). In that case, the defendants were licensed under an agreement with the plaintiffs to use certain trade secrets and know-how relating to lining tank cars. There was a post-termination restriction preventing the defendants from engaging in the business of lining tank cars in the whole of Canada for two years following termination. There was evidence that the defendants carried on business in only certain parts of Canada, and they claimed that the clause was too wide. In upholding the restraint, the court took into consideration the fact that the plaintiffs were subject to a similar restraint.

In English courts, on general principles, the rule that exclusive agency and similar agreements will be upheld will usually prevent the court from interfering on the restraint of trade ground so long as the restrictions do not unilaterally fetter the licensee for an unjustifiable period. It is also possible that the principle mentioned in *Esso Petroleum* v *Harper's Garage* — that agreements containing restrictions applicable only to goods sold under them fall outside the doctrine because the covenantor obtains only a limited right under the agreement, rather than giving up a right he already has, do not fall within the doctrine — may apply by analogy to prevent restrictions attached to a licence being affected by the doctrine. If such is not the case, however, a distinction may be drawn between anti-competitive restrictions expressed to continue after termination of the licence, for which there is usually little or no justification and which will therefore be regarded as a naked covenant in restraint of trade (*Vancouver Malt & Sake Brewing Co* v *Vancouver Breweries* (1934)), and those which specifically restrict use or disclosure of the confidential information, which might be expected to be upheld either by reference to the doctrine or under the breach of confidence rules. The Patents Act contains provisions aimed at preventing the patent owner from using his patent to extend his monopoly beyond the terms of the patent.

Restrictions attached to a licence may fall within the ambit of Article 85 and are dealt with in Chapter 7.

Chapter 6

Evaluating the restraint

1. Rules of construction

The first rule is that restraint clauses should be definite and clear (see, for example, *Davies* v *Davies* (1887); *Express Dairy Co* v *Jackson* (1930); *Commercial Plastics Ltd* v *Vincent* (1964)). A vague clause will fall foul of the principle against uncertainty.

The second rule is that the court must consider the restraint as at the date of the contract in the light of circumstances existing and what is likely to have been within the contemplation of the parties at that time. The reason for this is that a restraint clause is either valid or void *ab initio*. It cannot change its status as a result of the subsequent behaviour of the parties (there are dicta of Lord Denning to the contrary, but this seems to be the generally accepted view).

That said, it seems to be the court's choice whether it applies a literal or a liberal construction to the restraint clause. The literal approach can be seen in *British Reinforced Concrete Engineering Co* v *Schelff* (1921) (see Chapter 2), where the court construed a restraint in a business sale agreement as applying to the whole business of road reinforcements and not merely to "loop" road reinforcements, which was the extent of the business being sold, thus rendering the clause unenforceable. Similarly, in *Commercial Plastics Ltd* v *Vincent* (1965), an employer-employee case, a clause which contained no geographical limit was held to be worldwide and therefore unenforceable since the employer's business was confined to the United Kingdom. There are many more examples.

The judgment of Lopes LJ in *Moenich* v *Fenestre* (1892) has often been cited as a starting point for the liberal approach:

> "... you must construe the agreement according to the reasonable meaning of the words used without regard to what may be the effect of such construction."

This seemingly rather ambiguous statement is at the root of a line of authority which permits the court to examine the restraint in the light of other wording in the contract and the general circumstances of the case to ascertain the "true" meaning of the clause. Thus a clause which, if interpreted liberally, would be too wide, may be validated by a narrower interpretation.

This approach may be seen in the judgment of the Court of Appeal in *Marion White* v *Francis* (1972) where it was argued that the clause was too wide as it prohibited the defendant from being engaged in a capacity other than a ladies' hairdresser (Chapter 3). Similarly in *Home Counties Dairies Ltd* v *Skilton* (1970) it was argued that the clause prohibiting the supply of milk and "dairy produce" could prevent the defendant from taking employment with a shop or restaurant which supplied those products to customers of the ex-employer. The Court of Appeal again insisted firmly that the agreement must be construed in the context of the business in which the employee was actually engaged.

The courts themselves, it may be said, do not seem to recognise that there are two lines of authority or, at least, that there is any conflict between the two lines of authority. They reconcile them by applying a single rule to the effect that the clause must be interpreted in the context of the agreement and if a literal interpretation gives rise to ambiguity then other evidence may be let in to show what was within the parties' contemplation at the time the contract was made. Reading the cases, however, it is difficult to sustain the view that the ambiguity in cases where courts have taken a liberal view is any greater than in cases where the court has used the literal approach. The line taken in *Commercial Plastics Ltd* v *Vincent* may be contrasted with that taken in *Littlewoods Organisation* v *Harris*. It is true that, in the latter case, Lord Denning criticised the approach taken in the former on the ground that a covenant should not be invalidated simply because there are "unlikely or improbable contingencies" in which it might operate unreasonably, but it is submitted that the contingency in question in *Commercial Plastics Ltd* v *Vincent* was that the employee might have accepted work outside the United Kingdom and, since he could well have been forced to seek work outside the United Kingdom, it could not truly be described as either unlikely or improbable. Equally, the other judges in the Court of Appeal were not in agreement on the point. Nevertheless, even if *Commercial Plastics Ltd* v *Vincent* was wrongly decided, that still leaves standing other authorities which support the literal construction, not least among them being *British Reinforced Concrete Engineering Co Ltd v Schelff*. If one compares that case with *Littlewoods Organisation v Harris*, one might come to the conclusion that, on the face of it, there may be authority for saying that the literal (harsher) approach to construction is to be taken to business sale agreements while a more liberal approach may be taken with respect to restraints in contracts of employment. Clearly, this cannot be so since it would overturn a fundamental principle which has been central to the doctrine since the end of the last century. However, if that is not to be the practical effect, some way must be found of reconciling the two cases.

As Lord Denning pointed out in *Littlewoods Organisation v Harris*, the literal approach has its drawbacks. A restraint clause may be invalidated as too wide simply because it could be construed to include activities which were not within the contemplation of the parties at the time the contract was made. However, it is submitted that this argument can be criticised on two counts. First, it cannot be assumed that the covenantee had in mind only the prevention of activities which would compete with and damage his legitimate interests. Employers are not immune from the temptation to fetter their employees as tightly as possible; and if such an assumption were made, there would be little justification for the restraint doctrine at all. Secondly, the drafting of the covenant is in the hands of the covenantee. It is surely his task to ensure that he has the requisite protection. In all fairness, he ought to be taken to mean what he says and any ambiguity should be construed against him, as is the case with excluding and limiting terms. There may be grounds for drawing a distinction between "home-made" agreements, which perhaps ought to be construed more liberally (and if criticism of *Commercial Plastics Ltd v Vincent* is justifiable, it might well be on the ground that the agreement was in that case a "home-made" one), and professionally drawn agreements. Where a professional draftsman has been employed, the case for a literal construction is strengthened for, if the clause is drafted ambiguously and therefore fails, the covenantee ought to be able to recover damages from his legal adviser for negligence or breach of contract. There is no indication whether the agreement in *Littlewoods Organisation v Harris* was professionally drafted or not, and certainly the judges did not think it significant enough to refer to, but had the Littlewoods Organisation sought legal advice, their lawyers would surely have advised them that a restraint without geographical limitation was generally construed as a worldwide restraint and would, in relation to their business, be too wide. If Littlewoods failed to take legal advice on the restrictions, should the court have remedied the deficiency?

That said, the liberal approach is quite clearly the one which has won favour, at least with the Court of Appeal, over the last twenty years or so. (The attitude of the House of Lords to exclusive service contracts, however, may suggest that the climate of liberality has not extended to the higher court.) If the court takes the view that it can interpret the clause so as to restrict it to what is reasonable and enforceable, there are two ways in which it can alter the contract to achieve that effect. It may either read in limiting words, or it may strike out words which make the restriction too wide.

(a) Limiting words

In *Littlewoods Organisation* v *Harris* the court found itself able, on a construction of the agreement as a whole, to read in words limiting the restraint so as (i) to cover only the part of the Littlewoods business in which the employee was employed and (ii) to extend it no further than the United Kingdom. In doing so, the court relied *inter alia* upon the authority of a previous Court of Appeal case, *Home Counties Dairies Ltd* v *Skilton*. In that case, which concerned a non-solicitation and non-dealing covenant given by a milk roundsman which prevented him being involved in the sale of dairy produce for two years after termination of his employment, words limiting the covenant so that it would prevent the former milkman from selling only the relevant products in the employment of another dairyman were read into the agreement. However, it appears that the court exceeded the authority on which it relied. Harman LJ stated that covenants in restraint of trade must be limited to circumstances which the court considers the parties had within their contemplation when the contract was made, and cited as his authority a judgment of Sir Nathaniel Lindley which refers to "cases which may possibly arise" to which the restriction "cannot reasonably be applied" and which "cannot reasonably supposed ever to have been contemplated by the parties".

As with Lord Denning's criticism of the decision in *Commercial Plastics Ltd* v *Vincent* on a similar ground, it begs the question: were all the contingencies which might be considered too wide unlikely? The rule is not that where there are unlikely contingencies the court should read the contract so as to exclude them, but that unlikely contingencies should not *of themselves* be allowed to defeat the operation of the clause.

The "unlikely contingency" in *Skilton* was that it might prevent him from being employed in a restaurant which sold milk or a shop which sold cheese. Perhaps that was outside the parties' contemplation. Who knows? Harman LJ was firmly of the view that that was excluded from the ambit of the clause. But what about a shop in the same locality as the milk round, and which sold milk and dairy produce and also operated a delivery service? A literal construction of the wording of the clause would bring that situation within its ambit, but would a liberal construction? Whether that possibility would make the clause unreasonable is a question for the court to decide, but the contemplation of the parties, or to be more accurate the covenantee if it can be assessed at all, is surely not limited to employment with another dairyman but employment with any competitor and may well extend further.

In this case, then, since the covenantee's primary concern was to protect his trade, and his trade could be injured just as easily by a shop operating a delivery service as by a dairy company operating a milk round, it is submitted that it was not enough to read in the limiting words "in the business of a dairyman" as the court did, but to reflect the covenantee's true intentions it would have been necessary to read in the additional words "or any other competing business". Yet those words make any restraint too wide (compare *Nordenfelt*).

It is further submitted that by reading in the limiting words "in the business of a dairyman", the court was tailoring the restraint to prevent what actually happened rather than determining its *ab initio* effect.

The *Harris* case creates different problems, not least because there was little unanimity between the judges on the approach to be taken. In that case, which concerned a covenant restraining an employee from working for Littlewoods' major competitor, the competitor (GUS) had many subsidiaries worldwide concerned in a variety of businesses. The plaintiffs, Littlewoods, on the other hand, only had a chain of stores and a mail order business in the United Kingdom. Lord Denning (albeit on the authority of a previous decision of his own in the field of company law, which has been criticised in the House of Lords) thought that GUS and its subsidiaries were to be treated as a single entity so that the extension to subsidiaries was not unreasonably wide. He was further prepared to read in words limiting the covenant to the mail order business of GUS in the United Kingdom.

Megaw LJJ, on the other hand, did not consider *Commercial Plastics Ltd* v *Vincent* to be wrongly decided. He distinguished it, however, on the basis that in *Commercial Plastics* the agreement in question was accepted and properly to be construed as universal in its application. Nor did Megaw LJ take the same view as Lord Denning with regard to subsidiaries. Instead, on the authority of *Home Counties Dairies Ltd* v *Skilton* and *Plowman* v *Ash* (1964) he decided that the words "any company subsidiary thereto" could be interpreted to mean "any subsidiary which at any relevant moment of time during the period covered by the covenant is concerned wholly or partly in the mail order business carried on in the United Kingdom". He emphasised that he was not suggesting that the covenant be re-written but was interpreting it as he understood it ought to be interpreted in the circumstances.

Browne LJ (dissenting) agreed that it did not matter whether the business was carried on by subsidiaries or not. In his view (and he appeared to be impressed by the judgment in *Commercial Plastics Ltd* v *Vincent*) the clause was unreasonably wide as it would be unreasonable to prevent the defendant (as it would) from working for a GUS subsidiary in Canada. He seemed to feel that it was generally permissible to read words into a clause to give it a reasonable construction. In his view, however, the precedents cited were lent their strength only by the agreement in question having other clauses which expressly supported the construction given (the *Harris* agreement did not) and that to make the "elaborate" insertions required by Denning and Megaw LJJ would in fact be re-writing the agreement so as to make an unenforceable clause enforceable.

It is submitted that Browne LJ's judgment was more in line with previous authority than were the majority judgments. It also highlights an important point: even the majority were adamant that the court will not "re-write" the agreement for the parties but there is obviously a wide divergence of opinion on what amounts to re-writing. The wider problem is that the more liberally the court interprets the clause, the further it moves away from the doctrine. As stated earlier, the generally held view is that a clause is valid or void *ab initio*. This is a pure law doctrine: if, judged at the time the contract was made, the clause was too wide, the clause is bad. If it is not too wide, it is good. It is not a doctrine which is always easy to apply, but it does make for a degree of certainty. The new approach seems to involve looking *ex post facto* at what the covenantor has done, passing a moral judgement on him and reading words into the covenant so as to restrict exactly what has been done, retrospectively validating the covenant. This may not be what the judges admit to doing, but it is certainly the practical effect. As was noted in Chapter 3, by taking this approach, the court ceases to apply a pure law doctrine but admits equitable considerations – equitable considerations, moreover, which do not always appear to be fairly applied to the parties.

There is no indication in the earlier judgments that the defendant's actions are relevant to the application of the doctrine, even when general equitable principles are involved. Note, for instance, the approach taken to the evidence by Cross J in *Printers and Finishers Ltd* v *Holloway* where it was not in question that Holloway had acted quite improperly:

> "One naturally aproaches the problem in this case with some bias in favour of the plaintiffs because Holloway has shown himself unworthy of their trust; but to test their argument fairly one must take the case of an employee who has been guilty of no breach of contract."

This, it is submitted is the preferable approach. By admitting moral considerations, not only are the courts no longer applying the doctrine as it has been applied over the decades since *Nordenfelt* but they are also removing that degree of certainty which the strict application of the doctrine allows. How is it possible for a party to an agreement or his legal adviser to determine whether a restriction under an agreement is binding when its effect is to depend on some future moral assessment by the court of whether the covenantor ought to compete in a particular way or not?

Finally, it is submitted, this approach in relation to contracts of employment is totally inconsistent with previous authority on the strictness with which the court should approach the construction of restraint clauses. A business sale agreement may be judged by different standards because the parties are on equal footing, usually both legally advised, consideration is taken for the covenant etc. Yet the court did not even read in the single word "loop" in *British Reinforced Concrete Engineering Ltd* v *Schelff*. On the same basis, in *Lyne-Pirkis* v *Jones* (a partnership case), the covenant had to be read according to what it actually said, not what it might have been taken to mean. The judge considered it significant that the parties knew what the correct phrase was because they had already used it earlier in the agreement.

If such is the case for business sale and partnership agreements, it is surely even more important for the courts not to make assumptions about what the parties meant in employment contracts.

In *Mason* v *Provident Clothing and Supply Co Ltd* (1913), Lord Moulton warned of the tendency of employers to extract wide covenants secure in the knowledge that the employee could not afford to go to court, and expressed his belief that the court should not encourage employers, by using their knowledge of the law, to extract from the covenant the maximum reasonable covenant which they required. It is submitted that, notwithstanding legal aid, the danger is as substantial today as it was then. It is still true, as Lord Moulton said, that the real sanction behind wide covenants is that an employee will not expose himself to the cost of litigation if he fears that at the end of the day the court will merely cut down the covenant so that it covers what he has done and no more. If the courts are prepared to do that, an employee bound under an ambiguous restriction can never be quite sure what he is prevented from doing, and his choice may come down to unemployment or litigation. Employers for their part will naturally try their utmost to protect themselves against competition. It is cheaper and easier to keep a good employee through the sanction of a restrictive covenant than to offer him better salary and conditions. *Littlewoods Organisation* v *Harris* can be viewed as a competition for the services of a first-class employee which Littlewoods would otherwise have lost because they were not prepared to pay so high a price for his services. Should the courts be interfering in this kind of valid competition in the market place? Should an employee be the loser merely because he has been entrusted with information which he may have no intention of ever revealing?

The parties to an employment contract are not on equal footing. The employer has access to legal advice and his covenant will usually have been drafted by a lawyer. It is drafted for his protection and, if he cannot take care to get it right, why should the court re-draft it for him? Moreover the employee receives nothing in return for the covenant. An entrepreneur is expected to take reasonable risks, and it is within his power, through good business practices, to minimise damage which might occur to his business through the loss of an employee to a competitor. These arguments have been advanced many times in the past in support of strict interpretation, and one wonders why the courts have chosen to go against them now by using this particular form of interpretation. It is relevant here to consider whether the same approach is taken to the doctrine of severance.

(b) Severance

There is nothing new about the doctrine of severance. It has been defined as "the rejection from a contract of objectionable promises or the objectionable elements of a particular promise, and the retention of those promises or those parts of a particular promise that are valid" (*Law of Contract* by Cheshire and Fifoot). Its scope is therefore wider than contracts in restraint of trade. In relation to contracts in restraint of trade it may operate in two ways: either to cut out the restraint altogether, leaving the remainder of the contract valid, or to cut down the extent of the restraint, thus making it reasonable and enforceable. It is with the second of these that we are chiefly concerned here.

The first major example in the context of restraint of trade was in the *Nordenfelt* case, where the courts deleted the words at the end of the covenant which made it unreasonable: *"or in any business competing or liable to compete in any way with that for the time being carried on by the company"*.

The following cases also provide examples.

Bromley v *Smith* (1909): The plaintiff was a baker and the defendant his assistant. The agreement between them prohibited the latter for three years from leaving the plaintiff's service from engaging or being engaged in the business of *miller, baker, hay, straw or corn dealer, or restaurant keeper or in the manufacture of flour meal*. The defendant had in fact set up in a bakery business and the restraint as it stood was held to be too wide as the employer was concerned only in the business of bakery. It was held that all the stated trades except that of "baker" could be deleted from the clause and the clause would thereby be rendered reasonable.

Scorer v *Seymour Jones* (1966): The contract between an estate agent and his employee stated that after termination the employee would for three years be restrained from carrying on or being employed or interested in the business of an *auctioneer, surveyor or estate agent* within five miles of the employer's premises. The employee set up as an estate agent on his own account within the restricted area. The court held that the clause was severable and upheld the part relating to estate agency.

Price v *Green* (1847): The contract concerned the sale of a perfumery business in London. The clause restricted the vendor from carrying on a similar business within the cities of London or Westminster *or within the distance of 600 miles from the same respectively*. Again, the italicised words were severed leaving a restraint of reasonable extent.

There are many other examples, such as *Lucas & Co Ltd* v *Mitchell* where an anti-competition covenant was severed leaving a non-solicitation covenant to stand, and *Goldsoll* v *Goldman* (see Chapter 1) where a product not dealt in by the covenantee and a list of places to which the covenantee's business did not extend were deleted from a restraint clause making it reasonable. Severance has traditionally been the chief method (some may say the sole method) by which unreasonable clauses may be deemed reasonable, and it is to be borne in mind that older dicta about construction, such as that in *Moenich* v *Fenestre*, were given in the context of deletion rather than insertion of words. Too wide application of the doctrine has, however, been discouraged on a number of occasions, notably by Lord Moulton in *Mason* v *Provident Clothing & Supply Co Ltd*, who expressed the view that part of a covenant should not be enforced unless:

(i)   it is clearly severable; and

(ii)   the part to be taken out is of trivial importance, or merely technical, rather than being central to the clause.

Lord Moulton also believed that it would be wrong of the court to apply the doctrine of severance so as to assist an employer who had drafted an unreasonably wide covenant on purpose.

Perhaps mindful of this, the courts have subjected the doctrine to fairly strict regulation. First, the deletion of words must not alter the meaning of the clause in any way. In other words, the words deleted must effectively be a separate covenant from those which remain (*S Nevanas & Co Ltd* v *Walker and Foreman* (1914); *Attwood* v *Lamont* (1920)). This is sometimes called the "blue pencil" test. Secondly, what is deleted must be "of trivial importance, or merely technical and not a part of the main purport and substance of the clause" (*Mason* v *Provident Clothing and Supply Co Ltd*). Thirdly, the deletion of the words should not alter the nature of the contract (*Kenyon* v *Darwin Cotton Manufacturing Co* (1936)). Fourthly, the doctrine allows the court only to delete words; it does not allow insertion, rearrangements or substitution, as this would amount to re-drafting the contract (*Putsman* v *Taylor* (1927)).

Doubt has to some extent been cast on the fourth principle by *Littlewoods Organisation* v *Harris* and the facts of some cases (for example, *Scorer* v *Seymour Jones*; *Lucas & Co Ltd* v *Mitchell*) suggest that the second principle is not much observed.

In *Sadler* v *Imperial Life Assurance Co of Canada Ltd* the court summarised the modern approach to the doctrine by stating that an unreasonable provision might be severed leaving the reasonable part to stand provided that three conditions are satisfied:

(i) the unenforceable provision is capable of being removed without the necessity of adding to or modifying the wording of what remains;

(ii) the remaining terms continue to be supported by adequate consideration;

(iii) the removal of the unenforceable provision does not so change the character of the contract that it becomes not the sort of contract that the parties entered into at all.

The first and third principles mentioned above still therefore appear to be applicable. There is, however, one point which arises in connection with the first principle. In *Attwood* v *Lamont* the covenantor was employed as a head cutter and manager of the tailoring department of a departmental store. He signed an agreement saying that after termination he would not carry on the trades of *tailor, dressmaker, general draper, milliner, hatter, haberdasher, gentlemen's, ladies' or children's outfitter* (in short, all the businesses carried on in his employer's store), within the restricted area. He went into the business of tailoring within the restricted area and his ex-employer sought to have the covenant limited to tailoring and upheld as reasonable. The Court of Appeal refused to do this. It considered *inter alia* that the covenant was not several distinct covenants for separate businesses, but one covenant which covered all the businesses carried on by the ex-employer, and could not therefore be severed. In *Scorer* v *Seymour Jones*, however, the Court of Appeal did not agree with this distinction, and finally in *Lucas & Co Ltd* v *Mitchell* the Court of Appeal felt that the view in *Scorer* was the one that it should follow.

Distinctions have been drawn between these cases on the basis that the covenant in a business sale agreement should be subjected to the doctrine of severance more readily than a covenant in an employment contract. (See *Law of Contract* by Cheshire & Fifoot.)

(c) Relationship between the rules

The doctrine of severance is of more limited application than construction by the insertion of limiting words. It is also subject to stricter rules. It applies only where the covenantee is entitled to one thing but has clearly stipulated for two or more separate things. It is not that the clause is ambiguous but that the covenantor should be restricted to that which he is entitled on a literal interpretation of the clause. A great deal of care is taken not to "re-write" the agreement, ie not to alter its meaning. This is achieved by deleting only separate clauses. By contrast, although limiting words also cannot be used to "re-write" the agreement, they can be inserted so as to make substantial alterations going beyond what severance could achieve. It can be argued, of course, that there is not a great deal of practical difference between striking out the too-wide part of the covenant which extends to "the United Kingdom or any other part of the world" and reading into a covenant without geographical limitation words indicating that it extends only to the United Kingdom. If the court can do the former, why should it not be able to do the latter? Perhaps the distinction lies between the covenantor having indicated in the former case that he intended it to apply at least to the United Kingdom, but in the latter case, having given no indication at all where it is to apply, effectively leaves the court to decide for him *ex post facto*. A further distinction is that although it is usually fairly clear what may be taken out of a clause, one cannot forecast with any degree of certainty what the court might choose to read into it.

There is clearly a fine line between going against the fourth principle in the doctrine of severance and reading limiting words into an agreement; it seems inconsistent for the courts to be more willing to read words into a covenant than they are to delete words from it.

As a postscript, it is interesting to consider another drafting ploy which is apparently acceptable, at least to the Scottish courts. In *Hinton & Higgs (UK) Ltd* v *Murphy and Valentine* (1989) the defenders were former employees of the company. Clause 14 of their contract prohibited them from working for any previous or present client of the company without permission for at least eighteen months. Clause 15 provided that "the restrictions contained in Clause 14 are considered to be reasonable by the parties, but in the event that any such restriction shall be found to be void would be valid if some part thereof were deleted ... such restrictions shall apply with such modifications as may be necessary to make them valid or effective".

The Court of Session held that Clause 14 was too wide to be enforceable and allowed deletion of the words "previous or" as well as of restrictions (not quoted above) which would have made the contract unenforceable. The first part of Clause 15 was stated *obiter* to be "probably an illegitimate attempt to oust the jurisdiction of the court". The remainder was deemed to indicate that the parties were prepared to accept and abide by the restriction that the court by deletion decided was reasonable. The court was not re-writing the agreement, but was selecting the version of it which the parties had *inter alia* made with each other and was enabling the bargain as modified to stand.

The deletion of the words "previous or" was thus not made in accordance with the rules of severability (because they would not have amounted to a separate covenant) but in response to a clause inviting the court to alter the agreement and promising to abide by what the court thought to be reasonable. It is interesting to contemplate how far the courts might be prepared to take this idea. In this case what was required was merely the deletion of a couple of words, but the principle of selecting a reasonable version of the contract could well get out of hand. In *Baker* v *Hedgecock* (1888) the relevant restraint (in an employment contract) contained the words "any business whatsoever". The employee set up a tailoring business in competition and the plaintiff tailor asked the court to enforce the covenant to the extent that it was reasonable. The court refused, saying:

> "... if the covenant were, eg not to carry on a business in any part of the whole world, the court would be asked to uphold it by construing it as a covenant not to carry on business within, say, a limit of two miles, which would in effect be making a new covenant."

But is that not what the court was being asked to do in *Littlewoods Organisation* v *Harris?* Would the court's view in *Baker* v *Hedgecock* have been different if the employer had included a clause along the same lines as Clause 15 in the *Hinton & Higgs* contract?

2. Reasonableness

Having determined that the covenantee has an interest meriting protection, the court must decide whether the restraint is valid by testing its reasonableness or otherwise. As explained in Chapter 1, this test was originally formulated as a three-pronged test – that the restraint must be reasonable in the interest of both parties and the public interest. Very early on, the interests of the covenantor were subsumed into those of the public (see *Morris* v *Saxelby*) and the public interest was deemed to be served if the restraint was "no more than reasonably necessary to protect the interests of the covenantee" (for a modern discussion, see *Allied Dunbar (Frank Weisinger) Ltd* v *Frank Weisinger*). This has meant that judges have not often in modern times felt bound to justify their findings by reference to the public interest, as they did in earlier cases.

The onus of proof was batted back and forth between the covenantor and the covenantee in the late nineteenth century, Lindley LJ having stated in *Mills* v *Dunham* (1891) that all restraints are *prima facie* bad and it is up to the covenantee to show they are justified, while Romer LJ in *Haynes* v *Dorman* (1899) considered that it was up to the covenantor to show that the restraint went beyond what was reasonably necessary. The matter was still not absolutely clear after *Morris* v *Saxelby*, the formulations of their lordships in that case containing important differences. Lord Parker considered that Lord Macnaghten's judgment meant that the courts should not enforce contracts in restraint of trade unless there were special circumstances the proof of which was on the covenantee.

Lord Atkinson thought that it was up to the covenantee to establish that the covenant was reasonable while the covenantor had the burden of showing that it was injurious to the public interest.

Lord Shaw for his part considered that there were three stages to claiming an injunction on the basis of a covenant in restraint of trade:

(a) proving the clause in the agreement;

(b) proving facts and circumstances which warrant invocation of the law; and

(c) proving that such facts and circumstances are of sufficient weight to justify the setting aside of the presumption that the clause is void.

Lord Atkinson's formulation, however, has been generally accepted, and it is now the case that it is for the covenantee to show that the clause is reasonable in his own interests and for the covenantor to show that it is contrary to public interest.

Despite Lord Atkinson's formulation, the test of reasonableness which has been adopted means in practical terms that the covenantee will put forward evidence and argument to show that the protection afforded is no greater than necessary, and the covenantor will bring evidence to dispute that.

Although the court has in the past stated that the consideration paid by the covenantee is justification for the covenant (in business sale agreements at any rate), the court will not take into account the adequacy of the consideration in determining the reasonableness or otherwise of the covenant. In *Allied Dunbar (Frank Weisinger) Ltd* v *Frank Weisinger*, for example, the court was urged to take into account the fact that, if it upheld the clause it would be denying the defendant access to a market many thousands of times larger than the business which he had sold. Miller J dismissed this argument as a "novel and dangerous doctrine", or perhaps a revival of one which had long been discredited. In his view such an argument required the courts to undertake a balancing process which they were not really competent to do, and it was better left to the parties to do this by the usual process of negotiation.

Whether or not the clause is reasonable is a question of law for the court to decide, although it may hear evidence as to what is usual in the particular business in question. This being the case, the court is not bound by its previous decisions as to whether or not two years, say, is a reasonable time to bind a milkman. It is a matter for the judge to decide upon the appropriate evidence in the particular circumstances of the case before him whether a restraint is or is not unreasonable (*Dairy Crest Ltd* v *Pigott* (1989)).

Although reasonableness is undoubtedly a question of law, not fact (*Dowden* v *Pook Ltd* (1904); *Mason* v *Provident Clothing and Supply Co Ltd*; *Stenhouse Australia Ltd* v *Phillips* (1974), evidence may be given of the surrounding circumstances (*Peyton* v *Mindham* (1971)).

In the early days of the doctrine, the courts made a distinction between general and partial restraints, partial restraints being those limited in time or space or both. Partial restraints could be valid if reasonable but general restraints could never be valid. This rule was overturned in *Nordenfelt* v *Maxim Nordenfelt Guns and Ammunition Co* (1894). In that case, the defendant was a manufacturer of quick-firing guns and other weapons. The plaintiff was the purchaser of his business. Two years later the company agreed to employ the defendant as its managing director. There had been a restraint clause in the sale agreement which was amplified in the employment contract. The effect was that the defendant was restrained for twenty-five years (provided that the company remained in business that long) from otherwise engaging, either directly or indirectly, in the trade or business of a manufacturer of guns, gun mountings or carriages, gunpowder explosives or ammunition or in any business competing or liable to compete in any way with that for the time being carried on by the company. The restraint, despite being general in both time and space (it would probably have restrained the defendant for the rest of his working life from competing with the plaintiffs in any part of the world), was upheld apart from the final clause which was severed.

At this stage, the courts were still justifying their decisions with reference to the public interest, and the public interest in this case was that it was stated to "secure to England" the business and inventions of a foreigner and thus increased the trade of the country.

There is now no distinction between general and partial restraints: both are subject to the same test, although it is probably true to say that there are few instances of restraints which are general in all respects being upheld, and the covenantee who alleges that a general restraint is reasonable will usually have an uphill task.

Reference has already been made to the question of whether "reasonableness" and "fairness" are the same thing. The earliest cases spoke of fairness:

> "Wherever a sufficient consideration appears to make it a proper and useful contract, and such as cannot be set aside without injury to a fair contractor, it ought to be maintained."
> (Lord Macclesfield in *Mitchel* v *Reynolds* (1711).)

That the judges sometimes confuse "fairness" with "reasonableness" has been noted. More instances will be seen in this chapter. Although "reasonableness" and "fairness" sometimes coincide, they are not, it is submitted, always the same thing.

(a) Geographical area

The reasonableness or otherwise of the covenant in geographical terms is to be assessed in relation to the extent of the business to be protected.

Thus it is possible, as in *Nordenfelt*, to have a worldwide restraint where the business in question operates throughout the world. (Until *Littlewoods Organisation* v *Harris*, at least, it had always been assumed by the court that if a restraint does not expressly state a geographical limit, it is intended to be unlimited.) Similarly, restraints have been upheld extending to the whole of the eastern hemisphere (*Lamson Pneumatic Tube Co* v *Phillips* (1904)) and the whole of the United Kingdom (*E Underwood and Son Ltd* v *Barker* (1899)). Clauses which have been invalidated on the ground that the geographical area of the restraint is too wide are, however, far more numerous (eg *Attwood* v *Lamont*; *Mason* v *Provident Clothing and Supply Co Ltd*; *Leng & Co* v *Andrews* (1909); *Allsopp* v *Wheatcroft* (1872); *Empire Meat Co Ltd* v *Patrick* (1939); *Mallan* v *May* (1843)).

The court is, it seems, particularly severe in its assessment of a geographical limitation when it is a matter of an employee:

> "To preclude a former servant from carrying on his natural business in any part whatever of the United Kingdom is a very strong step and requires exceptional justification." (*S Nevanas & Co Ltd* v *Walker and Foreman* (1914).)

The general rule is that the greater the extent of area or duration, the greater the onus on the covenantee to prove that it is reasonable (*Morris* v *Saxelby*; *Attwood* v *Lamont*). It is not considered necessary for the covenantee to carry on business in every part of the area (*Connors Bros Ltd* v *Connors* (1940)) but the covenantee cannot protect areas into which he hopes to move at some time in the future. In *Beetham* v *Fraser* (1904) the court held that a clause restraining the covenantor from competing with the business of the covenantee at any address in future was void.

It seems that a larger area is permissible where customers are widely distributed (*Tallis* v *Tallis* (1853)) and it is possible to restrain a travelling salesman from representing a competitor in a wide area provided that the salesman serviced the whole of the area. In *Parsons* v *Cotterill* (1887) a traveller for a wine and spirit merchant was restrained from working for a competitor within a fifty mile radius, and this was held to be reasonable since the covenantee's business extended over the whole area. Similarly, a covenant was upheld in *Cussen* v *O'Connor* (1893) which restrained a traveller from travelling in a competing business in any county where he had travelled for the covenantee.

The court will not usually be so strict where it is a question of a business sale. As Lord Parker observed in *Morris* v *Saxelby*: "The covenant against competition is, therefore, reasonable if confined to the area within which it would in all probability enure to the injury of the purchaser."

The question of geographical area is particularly interesting in relation to multi-national companies with interests of different kinds in many parts of the world. So far, it does not appear that the courts have had to consider this problem, but a clue to the courts' probable attitude may be found in the approach of the Court of Appeal in *Littlewoods Organisation* v *Harris* discussed in more detail above.

The covenant may list the places in which the covenantee carries on business. In *Davies, Turner & Co* v *Lowell* (1891) the covenant was limited to "any business similar to the business now or hereafter carried on by the covenantee in London, Birmingham, Liverpool and New York and within fifty miles of each". The covenantee did no business in Birmingham but it was held that the word "Birmingham" could be severed from the covenant.

A covenant against solicitation will not normally be deemed unreasonable for geographical reasons because it is of necessity limited in its ambit to the area where the covenantee has its customers. It was contended in *Home Counties Dairies Ltd* v *Skilton* that both covenantor and customer might move to another area and so the restraint ought to be geographically limited to be valid. This contention was dismissed as "fantastical". Similarly in *Rannie* v *Irvine* (1844) a restraint on trading as a baker was upheld, it being no bar to upholding it that one customer might go to a village where the covenantor was the only baker.

In *Baines* v *Geary* (1887) a restraint on a milk carrier that he should not deal with "any of the customers served by or belonging at any time" to the covenantee was upheld. It was said that it amounted to two restraints, one in respect of customers who were customers during his term of employment and one in respect of other customers. The former was upheld and the latter was severed. In *Marshall & Murray Ltd* v *Jones* (1913) it was held that a non-solicitation covenant limited to customers served by and from a named dairy could not refer to business in another place.

(b) Duration

There are no hard and fast rules about customary lengths of duration. In *Dairy Crest Ltd* v *Pigott* the appeal was brought on the ground that the first instance judge had considered himself bound by earlier cases concerning milk roundsmen to the effect that a two-year restraint was not unreasonable, although his own view was that it was unreasonably long in the circumstances. The Court of Appeal considered that the judge had erred in principle. However, it is to be noted that in determining whether the duration of the two agreements was reasonable in *Esso Petroleum* v *Harper's Garage*, the judges were greatly influenced by periods which had been considered reasonable in other cases.

A restraint unlimited in time is deemed to be a lifelong restraint. Lifelong restraints, as has been shown above, can be imposed perhaps with less impunity than restraints unrestricted in space. In *Fitch* v *Dewes* (1921) for example, a solicitor's clerk was restrained from taking similar employment within a particular geographical area for the rest of his life. Similar restraints have been imposed on an estate agent and a baker's assistant.

The duration must be considered in relation to the geographical area and vice versa. The absence of a time limit will not make a covenant unreasonable if it is otherwise reasonable (*Chesman v Nainby* (1727)). In more recent times, it has been observed that restraints are not usually upset on the basis of duration alone. In *Bridge v Deacons* (1984) Lord Fraser, delivering judgment of the Privy Council, made it clear that the court was impressed by the fact that there was no reported case where a restriction which the court considered reasonable in all other respects had been held unreasonable on the basis purely of its duration.

It in fact seems from this and from other cases that the courts consider the parties to be the best judge of what is a reasonable duration (see, for example, *Allied Dunbar (Frank Weisinger) Ltd v Frank Weisinger* and *Marion White Ltd v Francis*).

There may perhaps be more reason to justify lifelong restraints than world-wide restraints: for example an employee may be in possession of a specific trade secret which might always be of use to a rival in the business. On the other hand, there are many pieces of confidential information which (as Neill J observed in *Faccenda Chicken v Fowler*) may remain confidential for only a limited time. It would not in that case be justifiable to impose a restraint extending beyond the time when the information might reasonably be considered confidential. The strength of a customer connection must dwindle with the passage of time, although this point does not appear to have been considered in the relevant cases.

Here again business sale agreements are given more liberal treatment, and in a number of cases long-term restraints have been upheld. In *Bryson v Whitehead* (1822), for example, a restraint for twenty years unlimited as to space was considered reasonable. A covenant may be taken to protect not only the covenantee but also his legatee, representative or assignee; such a covenant is not affected by the death of the covenantee or by his ceasing to carry on business (*Hastings v Whitley* (1848); *Elves v Crofts* (1850)).

Although the parties may be the best judges of what is reasonable – at least where they are on equal footing – a covenant which makes engaging in a competing business subject to the consent of the covenantee is unlikely to be upheld. In *Perls v Saalfield* (1892) a clerk to an oil importer covenanted that he would not take a situation or establish himself within fifteen miles of London without the consent of the covenantee, such consent not to be withheld if the covenantor proved to the covenantee's satisfaction that his new position had no connection with goods sold by the covenantee. This covenant was held to be void.

3. Interpretation of specific words and phrases

There are a number of words and phrases which have been specifically interpreted in the context of restraint of trade and these
are included by way of conclusion to this chapter.

In *Castelli* v *Middleton* (1901) the covenantor, a vendor of a business manufacturing vegetable colouring matter known as annato
and certain food preservatives, covenanted with his purchaser not
to compete in a similar business. He set up in the business of
manufacturing dairy utensils but also carried on a retailing business
to a small extent selling annato and preservatives which he bought
wholesale from the covenantee. It was held that the test of a similar
business is whether it is so like the other as seriously to compete
with it, and on the facts the covenantor was held to be in breach
of his covenant.

One phrase which crops up with regularity in covenants is "engaged
or concerned or interested in". A series of judgments have decided
that "interested in" in a restraint clause means having a proprietary
or pecuniary interest or being entitled to the profits of the business.
Thus assistants, managers and other employees are engaged or
concerned in the business but are not "interested" in it.

Where words are used to describe a business, they are given their
ordinary business meaning, for example, a merchant or dealer is
distinct from a manufacturer, but a wholesaler is not distinct from
a retailer (*Rogers* v *Maddocks* (1892)).

If an individual forms a company to carry on a business which
he is prohibited from carrying on, that will be caught equally as
much as if he carries on the business as a sole trader, but he does
not carry on a business belonging to and carried on in good faith
by his wife − even if he helps her or introduces her to customers
(*Smith* v *Hancock* (1894)). An employee does not "carry on" a
business at all, and is not "engaged in carrying on" a business
but, as mentioned above, he may be described as "engaging in" or
"being concerned in" a business. Being a creditor of a business is
not being "concerned" in it. The interpretation of "soliciting" was
discussed in Chapter 3. There is a distinction between soliciting and
"doing business" or "dealing" with customers and a covenantor
will not be in breach of a pure non-solicitation covenant by dealing
or doing business with former customers of the covenantee who
seek him out.

As regards geographical area and duration, months are taken to
be calendar months unless otherwise stated and miles and other
distances, unless otherwise defined, are assumed to be "as the crow

flies". Where a contract says that distance is to be measured by the "usual streets or approaches", any usual way will suffice — it does not have to be measured by the most frequented routes (*Atkyns v Kinnier* (1850)).

Chapter 7

Controlling trade restraints through legislation

The restrictions required by the client may go further than the restraint of trade doctrine and fall foul of legislation with more specific anti-restrictive aims. These rules will not apply in many instances but the draftsman should be aware of their existence. Each piece of legislation is sufficient in itself to be the subject of a separate volume and what follows is a broad summary of the legislation in operation. If an agreement is likely to be caught by any of these provisions, further research should be undertaken. Some further reading material is suggested at the end of the chapter.

1. The legislation

The legislation in question comprises the Restrictive Trade Practices Acts 1976 and 1977, the Competition Act 1980, the Resale Prices Act 1976 and Article 85 of the Treaty of Rome together with regulations made thereunder.

The restrictive trade practices legislation comprising the two Acts of that name and the Competition Act 1980 is designed to regulate collective agreements which have as their object price-fixing and/or the regulation of supply of goods and services. The 1976 Act is a consolidating statute, bringing together the Restrictive Trade Practices Act 1956, the Restrictive Trade Practices Act 1968 and the Fair Trading Act 1973. The full scope of this legislation goes beyond the kind of restrictions with which we are here concerned. The 1977 Act extends the scope of the 1976 Act, in particular with regard to provision of services. The legislation provides a procedure for registration of relevant agreements with the Director General of Fair Trading and for referral to the Restrictive Practices Court, a special body set up under the 1956 Act with powers of determining whether restrictions operate against the public interest.

The Competition Act 1980 permits the Director General of Fair Trading to enquire into anti-competitive practices of firms which are not caught by the Restrictive Trade Practices Act. The Director General can initiate preliminary enquiries and publish a report as to whether anti-competitive practices are involved. If he believes they are, referral to the Monopolies and Mergers Commission may follow or the Director General may instead take undertakings from the firms involved. If a referral is made, the Commission must investigate and report whether the practice is anti-competitive and whether it has operated or may be expected to operate against the public interest. On receipt of an adverse report, the Secretary of State may order the firm to desist or to modify its practice. The Act does not list anti-competitive practices but one common example is the refusal by manufacturers to supply goods to certain outlets, usually because they will be sold at a discount.

The Resale Prices Act 1976 is aimed specifically at suppliers of goods who attempt to control the price at which the goods may be re-sold to dealers. The Act provides a mechanism for referral to the Restrictive Practices Court which determines whether the restrictions operate against the public interest.

As regards the term "public interest" as it is used and determined in connection with the legislative provisions, this is a slightly different concept from public policy as interpreted in respect of the common law doctrine.

Articles 85 and 86 of the Treaty of Rome are aimed at agreements which have the effect of distorting competition within the European Economic Community. Their scope is wide; it should not be thought that they will apply only to international agreements, although their main relevance here is to contracts for European distributorships and cross-border franchising agreements.

2. Restrictive trade practices

The restrictive trade practices legislation came into being as a result of defects in the common law doctrine as a means of controlling restraints on competition. The main problem with the doctrine is, of course, that it develops on a case-by-case basis, and the court is unable to intervene where the parties carry out the agreement, even though public policy might be firmly against it and the interests of third parties might be damaged. A secondary problem is that, as demonstrated in earlier chapters, the public interest has to some extent been subsumed into the interests of the parties, and a restriction which is reasonable in the interests of the parties is likely to be upheld although it may have strong anti-competitive aims.

The present legislative provisions are now contained in the Restrictive Trade Practices Act 1976 (as amended by the Restrictive Trade Practices Act 1977 and the Competition Act 1980). The common law doctrine is not repealed but, in relation to agreements to which the legislative provisions apply, the legislation takes precedence by virtue of the fact that its provisions are more stringent than the common law tests and a restriction which fails the legislative tests is unlikely to be upheld under the common law rules.

The scheme of the Act is to make certain types of agreement registrable with the Director General of Fair Trading. It is then up to the Director to decide whether they are contrary to the public interest and, if so, to refer them to the Restrictive Practices Court.

An agreement is registrable if the parties are, or include, two or more persons (including companies and partnerships):

(a) carrying on business within the United Kingdom in the production, supply or processing of goods; or

(b) carrying on business within the United Kingdom in the supply of services,

and the agreement is one under which restrictions are accepted by two or more parties in respect of such matters as:

- the prices to be charged for goods;
- the charges to be made for services;
- the terms or conditions of supply;
- the persons to or for whom goods or services are to be supplied; and
- the areas or places in which goods or services are to be supplied.

The term "agreement" has a wide meaning and includes any agreement or arrangement whether in writing or not and whether or not it is intended to be legally enforceable.

A "restriction" includes any negative obligation (express or implied) which arises when a party to the agreement accepts some limitation on his freedom to make his own decisions about prices, charges or other matters in connection with the supply or acquisition of goods or services.

Information agreements, for example as to furnishing information in relation to selling prices or terms and conditions of sale, may be caught (s 7) even where they do not contain negative obligations, and there are special provisions aimed at including recommendations made by trade associations or services supply associations to their members, for example the provision of standard terms and conditions which members are expected to use.

There are, however, a large number of categories of agreement which are exempt from the operation of the Act. These include patent licences, bilateral exclusive dealing arrangements and terms relating to employment.

(a) Effect of default

An agreement to which the Act applies is void (s 35(1)) if particulars are not furnished to the Director General within the relevant time limits, that is to say:

(i)   before the restrictions take effect; or

(ii) if the operation of the restrictions is postponed for more than three months after the making of the agreement, within three months of the making of the agreement.

If any party who carries on business within the United Kingdom gives effect to or enforces or purports to enforce the provisions of a registrable agreement which has not been duly registered, the Director General may apply to the court for an order:

(i)   restraining the parties from giving effect to or enforcing or purporting to enforce the restictions; or

(ii) restraining the parties from giving effect to or enforcing or purporting to enforce the restrictions in any other registrable agreement, particulars of which have not been duly furnished for registration.

Giving effect to a void restriction is not a criminal offence but it is "unlawful" and any person who has suffered loss resulting from the operation of the restriction is empowered to bring a civil action to recover damages for breach of statutory duty (s 35(2)).

(b) Reference to the court

The Director General has a general duty to refer registered agreements to the Restrictive Trade Practices Court (s 1).

However, reference is discretionary in the following cases:

(i) Where the agreement or all the restrictions in it have been terminated or have ceased to have effect (s 21(1)(b)). However, the Director General may still refer the agreement if there is a risk of it being revived or another similar agreement being made.

(ii) Where, upon a representation made by the Secretary of State, the Director General has received a direction discharging him from referring the agreement because the restrictions are not of such significance as to call for investigation (s 21(2)).

In this context, "significance" means capable of causing detriment of which the court would be likely to take account if the agreement came before it.

(c) The role of the court

The court must consider each restriction in the agreement and decide whether it is contrary to the public interest. It does so with reference to criteria in the Act which are commonly called "gateways". These are contained in s 19 and may be summarised as follows:

(a) having regard to the character of the goods or services, the restrictions are reasonably necessary to protect the public against injury in respect of their use;

(b) the public, as purchasers, consumers or users would be denied other specific and substantial benefits and advantages if the restrictions were to be removed;

(c) the restrictions are reasonably necessary to counteract measures taken by a person not a party to the agreement with a view to preventing or restricting competition;

(d) the restrictions are reasonably necessary to enable the parties to the agreement to negotiate fair terms of supply from persons not parties to the agreement who control a preponderant part of the trade or business of supplying such goods or services;

(e) in the conditions actually obtaining or reasonably foreseeable, the removal of the restrictions would be likely to have a serious and persistent effect on the general level of unemployment;

(f) in the conditions actually obtaining or reasonably foreseeable, the removal of the restrictions would be likely to cause a reduction in the volume or earnings of substantial export business;

(g) the restrictions are reasonably required for the maintenance of other restrictions not found by the court to be contrary to the public interest;

(h) the restrictions do not directly or indirectly restrict or discourage competition to any material degree and are not likely to do so.

The restriction must meet at least one of these criteria; in addition the Restrictive Trade Practices Court must consider it not to be unreasonable, having regard to the balance between the matters established in connection with the "gateway" and any detriment to the public or persons not parties to the agreement resulting, or likely to result, from the operation of the restriction (ss 10 and 19 as amended).

In *Re Net Book Agreement, 1957* (1962), the agreement was a price-fixing agreement between publishers which provided that most of their books were not to be sold to the public at less than their net price. The agreement also imposed certain standard conditions of sale. The court found the agreement not to be against the public interest, applying gateway (b) − that the removal of the restrictions would deny the public other specific and substantial benefits − because the public benefit from a large number of specialist booksellers who can maintain an adequate stock rather than there being a small range of books sold at cut price from larger sellers of other goods. The public also benefit from a greater number of new titles. The court refused to accept that gateway (f) applied as the publishers could not establish that the volume of export earnings was sufficiently substantial.

3. Resale price maintenance

The Resale Prices Act 1976 contains provisions aimed against agreements between suppliers and dealers which provide for minimum prices at which goods may be re-sold. Part I deals with collective resale price maintenance and Part II with individual resale price maintenance.

Any term or condition in a contract for the sale of goods by a supplier (including a manufacturer or wholesaler) to a dealer (including a wholesaler or retailer) in respect of minimum resale prices is void (s 9). Furthermore, it is unlawful for the supplier to impose any such term or to notify dealers or publish details of minimum prices (recommended retail price excepted).

It is of course possible for a supplier to impose minimum resale prices by other than contractual means, for example by the withholding of supplies. This is prohibited by s 11. Withholding of supplies (s 12(1)) includes:

(a) refusing or failing to supply goods to the order of the dealer;

(b) refusing to supply goods to the dealer except at prices significantly less favourable than those at which he normally supplies to the other dealers;

(c) refusing to supply goods to the dealer on terms or conditions as to credit, discount or other matters, which are significantly less favourable than those on which he normally supplies to other dealers;

(d) treating him in a manner significantly less favourable than that in which he normally treats other dealers in respect of times or methods of delivery or other matters arising in the execution of the contract.

The supplier has a general defence if there are other grounds which, had they been the sole grounds, would have led him to withhold supplies (s 12(2)). In *Oxford Printing Co Ltd* v *Letraset* (1970) the defendants were sued on the grounds that they were withholding supplies, but they contended that their reason for withholding supplies was that the plaintiffs were not only cutting the price but were using the defendants' products to promote the sales of a rival. It was held that this was a good defence and the injunction was not granted.

There is also a general exemption in s 13 which allows a supplier lawfully to withhold supplies from a dealer if he has reasonable cause to believe that, within the previous twelve months, the dealer has used any goods of the same or a similar description as loss leaders.

Contravention of the resale price maintenance provisions is not a criminal offence but civil proceedings may be taken on behalf of the Crown to enforce compliance by injunction or for other appropriate relief. Persons affected by non-compliance may also bring proceedings for breach of statutory duty.

Under s 26, individual resale price maintenance is enforceable where goods are sold by the supplier subject to a condition which is not unlawful as to the price at which those goods may be resold. The supplier may enforce the condition against any person who is not party to the sale so long as he acquires the goods with notice of the condition.

Under s 14, the court may order that a particular class of goods be exempt from the provisions if the applicant can demonstrate to the court that the agreement passes through one of the following "gateways". He must show that in default of a system of maintained minimum resale prices applicable to the goods in question:

(a) the quality or varieties of the goods available for sale would be substantially reduced; or

(b) the number of retail establishments selling the goods would be substantially reduced; or

(c) the retail prices at which the goods are sold would in general and in the long run be increased; or

(d) the goods would be sold by retail to the public under conditions likely to cause danger to health in consequence of their misuse by consumers; or

(e) any necessary services provided in connection with or after the retail sale of the goods would cease or be substantially reduced,

and the detriment to the public of any of these must outweigh any detriment resulting from the maintenance of minimum resale prices. "Necessary services" under gateway (e) means services which, having regard to the character of the goods, are required to guard against the risk of injury, whether to persons or premises, in connection with the consumption, installation or use of the goods, or are otherwise reasonably necessary for the benefit of consumers or users (including any persons consuming or using in the course of business or for public purposes – ie not usually limited to the narrower, more usual, meaning of consumer).

It is notable that the instances in which a supplier has been able to persuade the court to exempt the agreement from the legislative provisions have been few indeed. Nevertheless, the case law on the subjects of restrictive trade practices and resale price maintenance is extensive.

4. Article 85 of the Treaty of Rome

The European Economic Community's competition policy, based on Article 3(f) of the Treaty of Rome, requires the institution of a system ensuring that competition in the common market is not distorted. This is supplemented by Articles 85 to 94. The purpose behind the policy is to back up the provisions for free movement of goods and services and freedom of establishment within the common market, and to encourage economic activity and maximise efficiency by enabling goods and services to flow freely among member states according to the operation of normal market forces. These aims can be seen to be wider than the more modest aims of the common law doctrine.

The EEC Commission, which is charged with the enforcement of the policy, has been subjected to considerable criticism by economists, lawyers and others for being too eager to strike down restrictions and for failing to distinguish between different types of restraints, and so recognise that while horizontal agreements between, for example, manufacturer and manufacturer frequently have undesirable anti-competitive results, vertical agreements between, for example, manufacturer and dealer often have desirable economic results, and, unlike the English courts in relation to the common law doctrine, for failing to distinguish between naked restraints and ancillary restraints.

Article 85, with which we are here primarily concerned, prohibits:

> "all agreements between undertakings, decisions by associations of undertakings and concerted practices which may affect trade between member States and which have as their object or effect the prevention, restriction or distortion of competition within the common market."

This can be broken down into three vital elements:

(i)   an agreement between undertakings, or a decision by an association of undertakings or a concerted practice;

(ii) the possibility of its affecting trade between member states; and

(iii) the object or effect of the agreement is to prevent, restrict or distort competition within the common market.

Article 85(1) goes on to specify five particular agreements, decisions or practices which are likely to be caught by the prohibition:

- (a) those which directly or indirectly fix purchase or selling prices or any other trading conditions;
- (b) those which limit or control production, markets, technical development, or investment;
- (c) those which share markets or sources of supply;
- (d) those which apply dissimilar conditions to equivalent transactions with other trading parties, thereby placing them at a competitive disadvantage;
- (e) those which make the conclusion of contracts subject to acceptance by the other parties of supplementary obligations which, by their nature or according to commercial usage, have no connection with the subject of such contracts.

Agreements etc which fall within any of the categories (a) to (e) will be *prima facie* deemed to infringe Article 85 subject to the significant effect on trade between member states being shown.

(a) Agreements, decisions and concerted practices

An agreement in the context of Article 85 does not necessarily mean a binding agreement. It must however be an agreement between "undertakings" and this has been interpreted very widely indeed. "Undertaking" includes any legal or natural person engaged in some form of economic or commercial activity (not necessarily in pursuit of profit) whether in the provision of goods or services, including cultural or sporting activities, banking, insurance and transport. The word comprises both public and private undertakings and even individual professionals. The undertakings who are parties to the agreement must, however, be independent of one another. Agreements between holding company and subsidiary will only infringe the Article if the subsidiary is fully independent. Similarly, agreements between a company and its employees will be held to fall outside the Article because employees are deemed to have no economic freedom.

"Decisions by an association of undertakings" include decisions by trade associations. Decisions do not need to be binding.

A "concerted practice" is a form of co-operation between undertakings which, without having reached the stage where an agreement proper has been concluded, knowingly substitutes practical co-operation between them for the risks of competition (*Imperial Chemical Industries* v *EC Commission* (1972)). It is sufficient ground for concluding that a concerted practice exists if each party has informed the other of the attitude it intends to take so that each can regulate its conduct safe in the knowledge that its competitors will act in the same way.

It is not necessary that the undertakings concerned operate in different parts of the European Community; purely domestic agreements have been held to affect trade between member states (*Brasserie de Haecht SA* v *Wilkin (No 1)* (1967); *Re Vacuum Interrupters Ltd* (1977); *Re Italian Flat Glass* (1989); *Salonia* v *Poidamani* (1980)).

(b) "Affecting trade between member states"

The test is whether, on the basis of objective legal or factual criteria, the agreement, decision or concerted practice allows one to expect that it will exercise a direct or indirect, actual or potential effect on the flow of trade between member states (*Société Technique Minière* v *Maschinenbau Ulm GmbH* (1966)).

What must be demonstrated is a deviation (actual or potential) from the normal pattern of trade which might exist between member states (*Etablissements Consten SA and Grundig-Verkaufs GmbH* v *EC Commission* (1966)).

It does not need to be shown that trade between member states has in fact been affected, or, it seems, even a strong likelihood that it will be affected. In *Pronuptia de Paris GmbH* v *Schillgalis* (1984), a case concerning a franchise, it was held that restricting the franchisee from operating outside the state territory could affect trade between member states even though the franchisee had never done so or had any intention of doing so in the future. This requirement, then, is not nearly so onerous as it seems.

The term "trade" includes all economic activities, including the supply of goods or services, broadcasting or communications generally, the exercise of intellectual property rights and the carrying on of any trade or profession.

(c) The object or effect on competition

In order to ascertain whether the agreement is capable of preventing, restricting or distorting competition, the Commission must examine the following (*Société Technique Minière* v *Maschinenbau Ulm GmbH* (1966)):

(i)   the nature and quantity of the products concerned, ie the parties' combined market share;

(ii)   the position and size of the parties concerned, ie the relative market share;

(iii)   the isolated nature of the agreement or its position in a series;

(iv)   the severity of the clauses;

(v)   the possibility of other commercial currents acting on the same products by means of re-imports and re-exports.

Obviously it will always be to some extent a question of scale as to whether an agreement, decision or practice is capable of affecting the market, and a *de minimis* principle (sometimes called the 5 per cent rule) has been introduced (*Volk* v *Etablissements Vervaecke Sprl* (1969)). Guidelines have been given as to the operation of this principle (less than 5 per cent of the total market in the area affected and an aggregate turnover of the undertakings involved of less than 200 million ecus), but these have no absolute legal effect and should be treated with caution.

(d) Infringement and its consequences

Paragraph 2 of the Article states that "any agreements or decisions prohibited pursuant to this Article shall be automatically void".

However it has been held (the *Consten/Grundig Case* (1966)) that only the parts of the agreement which infringe the Article are void, ie the restrictions are severable.

The Commission is charged with enforcement (Article 89) and it can take action of its own accord or on the instigation of a member or a private person, company or firm that thinks he or it is a victim of behaviour infringing Article 85. It is also empowered to carry out a "sector enquiry" (Article 12 Reg 17) if it considers that competition is distorted in a particular economic sector.

Regulation 17 of Article 11 gives wide powers to the Commission to obtain information. It is required first to serve a written request; if the information is not produced in response to the request, it can make a formal decision to order production. Fines may be levied for non-compliance at either stage.

Regulation 17 of Article 14 empowers the Commission to make investigations, and in particular:

* to examine books and records;
* to take copies of or extracts from books and records;

- to ask for oral explanations on the spot;
- to enter land, premises and vehicles.

However, before it can take any action such as imposing a fine, the Commission must give notice to the parties and allow them and any other interested parties to present their case.

Individuals or companies who have complained to the Commission and have had their complaint rejected may appeal to the European Court.

(e) Article 85 and English law

The Articles of the Treaty of Rome have direct effect in English law, and so an English court is empowered to decide whether an agreement infringes Article 85 or Article 86. For the action which it can take if it does find an infringement, see under Article 86 in the next chapter.

If the matter in question does not conform to the precise criteria of Article 85, it will of course fall outside the scope of Community law. However, there is clearly a degree of overlap between the Article and the doctrine in restraint of trade, and between the Article and the restrictive practices and resale price maintenance legislation. Where the matter could fall to be decided in accordance with either Community law or national law, Community law takes precedence. Thus, if an English court approves a restrictive practice, its approval will be of no effect if the practice is subsequently found to infringe Article 85. Complaint may be made direct to the Commission as well as to the English court. Similarly, an exemption under Article 85 will guarantee immunity from English restrictive practices or resale price law. The Restrictive Trade Practices Act 1976 gives a discretion to the Restrictive Practices Court to refrain from declaring an agreement contrary to the public interest where it infringes English law but not Article 85 or 86, and a separate discretion to the Director General of Fair Trading not to refer agreements to the Restrictive Practices Court if they have been approved by the Commission.

In an English court, a party may claim that an agreement is void for infringement of Article 85 and may be awarded an injunction or possibly damages (see under Article 86 in the following chapter).

5. Exemption from Article 85

Article 85(3) provides for the exemption of certain agreements as follows:

"The provisions of paragraph 1 may, however, be declared inapplicable in the case of:

- any agreement or category of agreements between undertakings;
- any decision or category of decisions by associations of undertakings;
- any concerted practice or category of concerted practices;

which contributes to improving the production or distribution of goods or to promoting technical or economic progress, while allowing consumers a fair share of the resulting benefit, and which does not:

(a) impose on the undertakings concerned restrictions which are not indispensable to the attainment of these objectives;

(b) afford such undertakings the possibility of eliminating competition in respect of a substantial part of the products in question."

Exemption will only be granted if an agreement is **notified** (see below).

As regards agreements which contribute to "improving the production or distribution of goods or promoting technical or economic progress" the following guidelines may be drawn from actual cases. Specialisation agreements, ie agreements by which manufacturers agree to stop duplicating manufacture and instead specialise in different products which they then exclusively supply to one another, can contribute to improving production by means of economies of scale. They can also improve technical progress, as for instance where manufacturers agree to collaborate on a new product in return for an exclusive supply agreement. An exclusive supply, dealership or distribution agreement can give benefits in terms of streamlining distributions and concentrating activities. It is not so clear what amounts to economic progress but it seems that an agreement which rationalises an operation and avoids duplication may contribute to its achievement (see the *Cecimo case* (1969)).

The benefit to the consumer will usually be in the form of lower prices, better goods or services or greater availability.

Restrictions (a) and (b) above are stringent; they go further than the "no further than reasonably necessary to protect an interest meriting protection" of the common law doctrine of restraint, although some of the same considerations may apply. The following two cases show how exemption can be obtained under Article 85(3).

The ACEC/Berliet Decision (1968): ACEC manufactured electrical transmissions for commercial vehicles, and Berliet were bus manufacturers. The agreement concerned the joint production of a prototype bus for which ACEC was to develop a new transmission system. ACEC undertook not to divulge to any other customer confidential information received from the latter and this was considered no more than was necessary in the light of the mutual confidence and risk involved.

The Carlsberg Brewery/Grand Metropolitan Decision (1985): Grand Metropolitan agreed to buy 50 per cent of its supplies of lager from the Carlsberg Brewery, the purpose being to enable Carlsberg to establish itself in the United Kingdom and build up an independent distribution network. Exemption was granted under Article 85(3).

(a) Block exemptions

Article 85(3) includes the possibility of block exemptions for whole categories of agreement or individual exemptions for particular agreements.

The advantage of block (or bloc) exemptions is that they cut down the Commission's workload considerably; they are also of assistance to those making agreements which might be caught by Article 85. Block exemptions have been made for a number of categories of agreement:

- patent licensing agreements;
- know-how licensing agreements;
- franchising agreements;
- specialisation agreements;
- exclusive supply and distribution agreements;
- exclusive purchasing agreements;
- motor vehicle distribution and servicing agreements.

These exemptions are made by Regulation and do two things:

(i) they define the clauses which may be included without loss of exemption ("the white list"); and

(ii) they define clauses which, if included, will result in loss of exemption ("the black list").

Although it is not possible to consider block exemptions in detail, a few words may be said about some of them.

Exclusive purchasing and distribution agreements: In EEC law the advantages to the consumer of an efficient distribution network based on exclusive purchasing and distribution agreements are seen to outweigh the anti-competitive nature of the restrictions they entail.

In respect of *exclusive distribution agreements* the white list includes the following restrictions:

(i)   an obligation on the supplier not to supply contract goods to resellers or users in the contract territory;

(ii)   obligations on the distributor:

- not to manufacture or distribute competing goods;

- to obtain contract goods from only the supplier;

- to refrain (outside the contract territory and in relation to contract goods) from seeking customers, establishing any branch and maintaining any distribution depot.

Clauses on the black list are aimed particularly at restrictions on parallel trading which is seen as having very beneficial effects on competition. They include:

- clauses restricting the distributor from exporting the goods by way of unsolicited sales;

- clauses which prevent intermediaries or users (for example by using trade marks or other industrial property rights) from obtaining goods from dealers inside the Community (or outside if there is no other source of supply).

Franchising: The white list for franchising agreements includes:

- protection of know-how; and

- honouring of guarantees.

The black list includes restrictions aimed at prohibiting the franchisee from:

- purchasing the franchised goods from other franchisees or from the franchisor's own authorised distributors;

- obtaining supplies of "incidental" goods (rather than the basic product) of equivalent quality to those offered by the franchisor;

- supplying any end user on account of his place of residence;
- using know-how after termination where it has come into the public domain otherwise than by the franchisee's own action.

The franchising exemption extends only to distribution and servicing, not to manufacturing franchises.

If the agreement seeks to include a clause which is not included in the white list for the category of agreement, individual exemption will have to be applied for.

For *patent licensing agreements, specialisation agreements* and *research and development agreements*, there is a third category of clause, the "grey restriction", and a special procedure ("the opposition procedure") must be undertaken in respect of them. If it is desired to include a grey restriction, the Commission must be notified; if it is not opposed within six months, it is deemed to be exempt.

There are also provisions in some categories as to market share and other conditions which might take the agreement out of the exempt category.

(b) Individual exemptions

The Commission is the only body empowered to grant an individual exemption, subject to a right of appeal to the European Court. The application procedure is to notify the Commission (see below) using Form A/B. In doing so the parties are required to indicate how the conditions for exemption under Article 85(3) are satisfied.

The Commission has indicated that it does not consider the purposes below to be restrictive of competition, ie if the sole object of the agreement is with regard to any of the following:

- exchange of opinion or research;
- joint market research;
- joint execution of comparative studies of enterprises or economic sectors;
- joint preparation of statistics and standardised calculation systems;
- co-operation in accounting matters;
- joint provision of credit guarantees;

- joint agencies for the collection of debts;
- joint agencies for advising on business organisation or tax matters;
- joint research and development;
- joint placing of research and development contracts;
- sharing of research and development projects between participating enterprises;
- joint use of production, storage and transport facilities;
- joint execution of orders, where the parties do not compete in the particular activity or could not execute the orders alone;
- joint selling arrangements, where the parties do not compete;
- joint after-sales and repair servicing, where the parties do not compete;
- joint advertising;
- joint use of quality marks.

However, if in doubt, negative clearance should be sought as it cannot always be assumed that such agreements do not infringe Article 85(1) (see *Notice Concerning Co-operation between Enterprises* (July 1968)).

(c) Notification and negative clearance

The notification procedure is as indicated in the preceding paragraph. It is essential to the obtaining of individual exemption and is sometimes called the "negative clearance procedure" as it requests the Commission to declare that the agreement does not fall within Article 85(1) or to grant an exemption. If the exemption is granted, it takes effect retrospectively as from the date of notification. This is important as it confers immunity to fines and temporary validity. The parties obtain immunity from fines in respect of anything done after notification provided that what is done is within what is notified (Article 15 Reg 17). Once notified, the agreement remains valid until the Commission decides that it infringes Article 85(1). The effect is that it is legally enforceable and parties are immune from private suit. Once an adverse decision has been made, however, validity is lost not only for the future but also for the period between notification and decision. The parties are not immune from fines if the Commission, after a preliminary examination, informs them that Article 85(1) has been infringed. There are also fines for intentionally or negligently supplying incorrect or misleading information.

There are six categories of agreement which need not be notified:

(i)   where all the parties belong to one member state and the agreement relates neither to imports nor to exports between member states;

(ii) two-party resale price maintenance agreements, ie agreements which only restrict the prices and terms on which the buyer can resell;

(iii) two-party agreements relating to the use of industrial property rights, eg patents, trade marks, know-how, designs;

(iv) agreements irrespective of the number of parties, concerned exclusively with developing standards or types or with their uniform application;

(v)   agreements irrespective of the number of parties, concerned exclusively with joint research and development;

(vi) agreements irrespective of the number of parties, concerned solely with specialisation where certain size criteria are satisfied, ie the goods to which the agreement relates do not exceed 15 per cent of the particular market and the parties' turnover does not exceed 200 millon units of account.

If the agreement falls within one of these categories, the parties do not have to notify *but may do so if they wish*. An agreement which falls within one of these categories and which is not notified remains fully valid until such time as it has been declared invalid (*Bilger* v *Jehle* (1970)). *It does not mean that it will never be found to infringe Article 85.*

(d) Comfort letters

The notification procedure being a fairly lengthy process, the parties may seek a "comfort letter" from the Commission which states that the Commission does not believe there is any need to take action because the agreement falls outside Article 85(1) or may be exempted under Article 85(3). The letter is not equivalent to exemption; an exemption may not be granted if there is a change of circumstances or if information supplied is incorrect. As explained above, an exemption will have effect in relation to national as well as EEC law, but the legal status of a comfort letter in regard to national law is uncertain.

6. Case examples

The body of case law is enormous, as one might expect, and the reader is directed to specialist works on the subject. The following cases are provided by way of illustration.

The Consten/Grundig Case (1964): The agreement between the parties appointed Consten exclusive distributor for Grundig in France for certain goods. In France Grundig was to sell only to Consten, and Grundig's distributors in other countries were restrained from selling outside their areas. Consten, for its part, agreed not to deal in competing goods or to sell outside France. The Commission held that the agreement infringed Article 85. The European Court upheld the Commission's decision to the extent that the restrictions were void.

This case provides a classic example of an Article 85 infringement. There was an agreement between undertakings. Its intention was to reserve to the two parties trade in the goods between France and Germany and it was therefore capable of affecting inter-member trade. The agreement was also designed to restrict competition. Clearly there was a breach of Article 85(1). As Consten's prices in France were higher than in Germany, the consumers were not being given a fair share of the benefits. And not all the restrictions were necessary, either to enable forecasting of future requirements or for servicing the guarantee obligations. Hence the agreement did not qualify for exemption under Article 85(3).

Ford Werke AG and Ford of Europe Inc v *EC Commission* (1984): This case concerned a Ford standard distribution agreement which, on the face of it, was perfectly acceptable. However, Ford was refusing to supply existing distributors in Germany with right-hand drive cars for export to England. The reason appeared to be that Ford wished to maintain an artificial partitioning of the market so that there would be different pricing levels in different member states. The Commission therefore refused to exempt the agreement and the European Court upheld the Commission's decision on the ground that this refusal to supply was part of the contract, albeit a tacit part, between Ford and its dealers. Becoming a Ford dealer meant acceptance of Ford's pricing policy, even without express agreement.

This case is included to demonstrate how far the European Commission and Court will go to uphold the spirit of the legislation. It shows how restrictions which are not expressed, or even implied in the usual sense, in the agreement can block the agreement from being exempted under Article 85(3).

The Roofing Felt Case (1986) and *The Meldoc Case* (1986): These were both cases of price-fixing cartels. In the first, seven manufacturers of roofing felt supplying the Belgian market entered into an agreement which included minimum price clauses, a ban on gifts to customers and a market quota system. There were also defensive measures aimed at preventing competition from imports. In the second, a number of dairy companies in the Netherlands agreed to price-fixing restrictions, a market quota and other provisions similar to those in the *Roofing Felt* case. The Commission investigated both cases, and very heavy fines were levied on the companies in question.

The Pronuptia Case (1984): In this case, the court was able to consider a franchising agreement in its entirety. The court's observations are interesting. While certain conditions concerning territory were held to be void (see above), others were upheld, including:

- standardisation provisions as to shop layout and fittings;
- a requirement on the franchise to purchase 80 per cent of its dress stock from Pronuptia and the rest from suppliers approved by Pronuptia;
- an obligation to hold minimum stocks.

The Commission considered that certain "qualitative" restrictions were essential to a franchising agreement. In the *Pronuptia Case* and the *Computerland Europe SA Case* (1989) the Commission held that a restriction on the franchisee's rights to "open up" other franchisees' territories was to be allowed under Article 85(3) as its tendency was to protect the franchisee's investment.

7. Conclusions

The following points should be borne in mind with regard to Article 85 generally:

- Article 85 does not apply to restrictions in contracts of employment.
- Article 85 may apply to any other kind of agreement, including business sales and mergers, distribution and agency, franchising or solus agreements and patent, trade mark and know-how licences.
- If the agreement is within a category exempted under a block exemption, it may contain only restrictions on the

"white" list and must not contain any of the restrictions on the "black" list.

- If the agreement is not within a category exempted under a block exemption, or if it is within such a category but contains other than permitted restrictions, the agreement as a whole should be considered in the light of surrounding circumstances to ascertain whether it could fall within Article 85(1).

- If there is a reasonable probability that the agreement falls within Article 85, it may be discussed with the Competition Directorate of the Commission (DG IV).

- If the agreement cannot be modified so as to avoid Article 85(1) and, in any event, if there is any real doubt as to whether it is outside the scope of the Article, notification should be made and negative clearance or a comfort letter obtained.

Further reading:

EEC Competition Law (Oxford University Press, 1988) by DG Goyder

Restrictive Trade Practices — a guide for members of the business community and their professional advisers (Office of Fair Trading, 1990).

Chapter 8

Controlling monopolies

1. Attitude of the courts

The earliest function of the restraint doctrine, as was noted in Chapter 1, was the control of monopolies. The public interest is said to lie in there being a number of competitors in the market rather than one or a handful of business organisations which control the market. Where the latter is the case, the following monopolistic effects may be seen:

(a) restriction of output to maximise profits and keep prices high;

(b) narrowing of choice for consumers;

(c) stifling of innovation which might result in greater efficiency/lower prices.

Any of these effects is clearly bad for the consumer and therefore likely to be against the public interest. A monopoly may be created in a number of different ways. One of the most common is for two or more business organisations manufacturing or retailing similar goods or supplying similar services to merge, or for one to take over the others. A business organisation might also merge with or take over its suppliers or distributors, thus securing for itself a stable source of supply, or a secure outlet for distribution.

However, there may be reasons why such a merger or takeover is impossible or undesirable. The business organisation in question might then achieve the same effect by making agreements with its peers or with its suppliers or distributors. Some of these agreements tie the other party with exclusive purchasing or exclusive selling clauses, and the application of the restraint doctrine was discussed in connection with these in Chapter 5. Agreements in the former category will usually be vendor-purchaser agreements and subject to the rules of the doctrine explained in Chapter 2.

Nevertheless, not all such agreements create or have a tendency to create a monopoly. Nor do agreements which have a monopolistic effect necessarily fall within one of these categories.

The court's traditional attitude, so far as the restraint doctrine was concerned, was not to favour monopolies, but their thinking on this subject has not been entirely clear, probably because the agreements brought to their attention were not in themselves monopolistic but might have tended, if taken with other similar agreements, to have a monopolistic effect. It is the anti-competitive nature within a relatively small field that has therefore occupied most of the judgments. Moreover, the early emergence of the "reasonableness" requirement prevented the courts from striking at clauses in agreements which might well have been monopolistic in effect but which did not appear to be unreasonable in themselves. In *North-Western Salt Co* v *Electrolytic Alkali Co Ltd* (1914), for example, the court upheld restrictions in a distributors' agreement for the sale of salt which purported to regulate prices, the amount to be sold, discounts, customers etc. Viscount Haldane said:

> " ... when the question is one of the validity of a commercial agreement for regulating their trade relations entered into between two firms or companies, the law adopts a somewhat different attitude – it still looks carefully to the interest of the public but regards the parties as the best judge of what is reasonable as between themselves."

Similarly, in *Attorney-General of the Commonwealth of Australia* v *Adelaide Steamship Co Ltd* (1913), Lord Parker said:

> "Monopolies and contracts in restraint of trade have this in common, that they both, if enforced, involve a derogation from the common law right in virtue of which any member of the community may exercise any trade or business he pleases ... "

Nevertheless, the Privy Council upheld the restraint in question and made the point that it was not aware of any case in which a restraint reasonable in the interests of the parties had been held unenforceable because it involved some injury to the public. In *McEllistrim* v *Ballymacelligott Co-operative Agricultural and Dairy Society* (1919) Lord Birkenhead said that was not to be taken to indicate that the two tests (ie the public interest test as well as the parties' interest test) were not still in existence.

Be that as it may, it seems that in *McEllistrim* the court was concerned more with the fact that the restrictions unilaterally fettered the covenantor rather than with any wider concern of the public about monopolistic trade associations. And in *English Hop Growers Association* v *Dering* (1928) a similarly restrictive agreement between a trade association and its members was upheld mainly because 95 per cent of the hop growers had agreed to it. The court seemed to feel that this satisfied the public interest requirements, although it might have been argued that the wider public interest was not served by 95 per cent of all hop distribution being under the monopolistic control of a single body.

To ascertain the modern attitude of the courts to monopolies in restraint of trade, we must go back to the solus agreement cases. Lord Morris commented in *Esso Petroleum* v *Harper's Garage* [1968] AC 269 at page 304 that "monopolies have always been in disfavour with the law", but like Viscount Haldane above he refers to them in such a way as to indicate that they are separate from restraints of trade. Yet restraint of trade can certainly lead to the creation of a monopoly. The solus agreements were not seen to be of themselves anti-competitive because, as is clear from Lord Denning's judgment in *Petrofina (Great Britain) Ltd* v *Martin* (1966) the petrol companies had to compete amongst themselves for the garage owners' business, and so garage owners did not have to tie themselves to unreasonable restraints in order to obtain their supplies. The judges in the House of Lords appeared to accept that the restraints were in the public interest as well as the parties' interests in that they produced an efficient and stable distribution network.

Much has been made, too, of *Vancouver Malt & Sake Brewing Co Ltd* v *Vancouver Breweries Co Ltd* (1934) which, it will be recalled, concerned restrictions on brewing beer which were contained in a brewer's licence, the court taking the view that since the vendors had never brewed beer it was a naked anti-competitive covenant. However, this decision can also be explained on the basis of reasonableness between the parties rather than any anti-monopolistic concerns the public might have. The more recent "exclusive services" cases, *Schroeder Music Publishing Co* v *Macaulay* and *Clifford Davies Management Ltd* v *WEA Records Ltd*, which involved a company having a monopoly over a songwriter's copyrights – whether or not there was any monopolistic intention to corner a particular market – were nevertheless decided purely on the basis of inequality of bargaining power between the parties rather than any wider principle.

The Canadian courts seem to have taken a wider view. In *Baker* v *Lintott* (1981) a lower court held that a covenant between a medical practitioner and his partners that he would not compete within a particular area for two years was held to be against the public interest in that it unduly restricted access of the public to his services – this decision was reversed on appeal. In another case, it was argued that a covenant was against the public interest as it had monopolistic tendencies. Although the covenant was not struck down, the Supreme Court seemed to accept the contention (see *Doerner* v *Bliss & Laughlin Industries Inc* (1890), and for a discussion of the Canadian courts' attitude to the public interest test see *Tank Lining Corporation* v *Dunlop Industrial Ltd* (1982)).

The attitude of the English courts has, however, been half-hearted, and the fact that they have in recent decades subsumed the public interest requirement into the parties' interest requirement has meant that the restraint doctrine has not proved an effective instrument for the control of monopolies. It has therefore been left to Parliament to enact provisions aimed at curbing the monopolistic tendencies of business organisations. This has, until recently, been done in a fairly desultory manner. The control of monopolies is, of course, something of a political "hot potato". Governments of both right and left have reason to deplore monopolies: the former because they are contrary to the principles of a free market, the latter because they make life more difficult for the consumer. Yet there are other considerations for both sides: a free market also dictates that the commercial organisations be free to conduct their business operations with as little restriction or intervention as possible (in fact, the traditional dilemma in which the courts have found themselves involved) while supporters of the left, having accepted that state monopolies are in the public interest, find it difficult to argue that private monopolies are not. Added to this, of course, is the problem that in many industries there are a few large suppliers who have such enormous economic power that they are very difficult to restrain. The control of monopolies is not, therefore, merely a matter of law, and it is not surprising that the courts have failed to involve themselves too closely in it.

2. The legislation

Control of monopolies in the United Kingdom is achieved partly through the restrictive trade practices legislation (discussed in detail in Chapter 7), which requires agreements containing certain types of restriction to be registered with the Director General of Fair Trading who may refer them to the Restrictive Practices Court. Partly it is achieved through control of mergers in the public interest under the Fair Trading Act 1973. Merger control is outside the scope of this book but it is worth noting in passing that mergers (other than newspaper mergers, which are subject to special rules) are likely to be referred to the Monopolies and Mergers Commission if two or more enterprises (at least one of which is carried on in the United Kingdom or controlled by a body incorporated in the United Kingdom) cease to be distinct and either (a) the value of the assets taken over exceeds £30 million, or (b) if the merger results in or enhances a "monopoly situation" with regard to the supply of goods or services. A "monopoly situation" is regarded as existing for this purpose if, in relation to goods or services of any description, at least 25 per cent of the total supply in the United Kingdom or in a substantial part of the United Kingdom are supplied either by or to one person, or by or to the persons by whom the enterprises are carried on which have ceased to be distinct.

3. Article 86 of the Treaty of Rome

There is also a possibility of any agreement which may have monopolistic tendencies being subject to the EEC legislation. Article 85 of the Treaty of Rome, which deals with clauses in agreements which affect competition, has been considered in detail in Chapter 7. There is, however, Article 86 of the Treaty still to be considered; Article 86 is designed to strike more closely at monopolies and their abuse of position.

Article 86 provides:

> "Any abuse by one or more undertakings of a dominant position within the Common Market or in a substantial part of it shall be prohibited as incompatible with the Common Market in so far as it may affect trade between Member States. Such abuse may, in particular, consist in:
>
> (a) directly or indirectly imposing unfair purchase or selling prices or other unfair trading conditions;
>
> (b) limiting production, markets, or technical development to the prejudice of consumers;
>
> (c) applying dissimilar conditions to equivalent transactions with other trading parties, thereby placing them at a competitive disadvantage;

(d) making the conclusion of contracts subject to acceptance by the other parties of supplementary obligations which, by their nature or according to commercial usage, have no connection with the subject of such contracts."

The scope of the Article is clearly very wide. As well as striking at mergers (although it was not until the *Continental Can* case in 1972 that the European Court confirmed that the Article applied to mergers and acquisitions), it can be used to strike at restrictions in the kind of agreement we have identified as being subject to the restraint doctrine. Although there is considerable overlap with the doctrine, Article 86 can be used to strike at restrictions which the courts have traditionally found unobjectionable under the doctrine. The Article applies also to some matters which are not covered by the restrictive trade practices legislation.

The conditions which are required for a breach are:

(a) there must be one or more undertakings involved (for the wide definition of "undertaking" see Chapter 7);

(b) the undertakings, or one of them, must hold a dominant position;

(c) the dominant position is within the Common Market or a substantial part of it;

(d) the undertaking must have abused its dominant position;

(e) the abuse must be capable of affecting inter-member trade.

Like Article 85, Article 86 does not catch contracts in restraint which do not affect inter-member trade; and, of course, the undertaking(s) in question must have a "dominant position" within the "relevant market" for the Article to bite.

It is therefore necessary to look first to see what is the relevant market and then establish whether the undertaking in question has a dominant position within it. Establishing the relevant market may seem easy but it is not always a straightforward task. In the *Continental Can* case, for example, the undertaking in question was a US manufacturer operating an international business making metal packages, packing materials and packaging machines. It acquired a West German subsidiary which had a high share in West Germany of the market in cans for various preserved foods and in metal caps for glass jars. Through another subsidiary, Continental Can agreed to purchase a controlling interest in a Dutch company which was the largest manufacturer of metal containers in the Belgium, Netherlands and Luxembourg area. The Commission's ruling was that Continental Can had acquired a dominant market position through the West German company, and that the acquisition of the Dutch company was therefore an abuse of this dominant position contrary to Article 86. In the event, the European Court overruled the decision. The court's decision was based on the ground that the Commission had failed to prove that there was a relevant market in which the Continental Can company had achieved a dominant position.

There are tests for establishing the relevant market. The "substitution" test (which depends on the substantial interchangeability of products) was proposed in *Istituto Chemioterapico Italiano SpA and Commercial Solvents Corporation* v *EC Commission* (1974). In order to establish that the products in the market are "substantially interchangeable", it poses two questions:

(i)   To what extent is the customer, importer or wholesaler able to purchase goods, products or services similar to those supplied by the undertaking in question or acceptable to him as substitutes?

(ii)   To what extent are other firms able to supply or capable of producing or supplying acceptable substitutes?

In answering the questions, the court takes into consideration the characteristics of the product, its price and the use to which it is to be put. It was this test that the Commission was criticised by the court for failing to apply in the *Continental Can* case.

There is also the "suitability" test. This was mentioned in *Continental Can*, and involves asking whether the products are "individualised" not merely by their being put to a certain use but by particular production characteristics which make them specifically suitable for a particular purpose.

There is also the *geographical* dimension of the market to be ascertained. The whole of the European Community may be the relevant market in geographical terms (*AKZO Chemie BV* v *EC Commission* (1986)). However, the relevant market may be one particular member state only (*General Motors Continental NV* v *EC Commission* (1975)). Even part of the state may form the relevant market.

A relevant market may also have a *temporal* dimension. There may for instance be a particular time of year or a particular period when substitute products are or were hard to come by (*Re ABG Oil* (1977)).

Having established the relevant market, it is necessary to decide whether the undertaking in question holds a dominant position in it. To some extent, these questions are interrelated. A dominant position was defined by the European Court in *United Brands Co and United Brands Continentaal BV v EC Commission* (1976) as:

"a position of economic strength enjoyed by an undertaking which enables it to prevent effective competition being maintained on the relevant market by giving it the power to behave to an appreciable extent independently of its competitors, customers, and ultimately of its consumers."

In *AKZO Chemie BV* (1986), the European Court said:

"The power to exclude effective competition is not ... in all cases coterminous with independence from competitive factors but may also involve the ability to eliminate or seriously weaken existing competitors or to prevent potential competitors from entering the market."

In the *Continental Can* case, the Commission explained "dominant position" as follows:

"Undertakings are in a dominant position when they have the power to behave independently, which puts them in a position to act without taking into account their competitors, purchasers or suppliers."

Characteristics of a dominant position therefore include:

(i)   power to exclude or weaken competition; and
(ii) power to act independently.

The following factors will be taken into consideration in determining whether there is in fact a dominant position:

- the market share held by the undertaking. This may be the most important factor where the share is over 50 per cent; where the share is lower, the nature of the market will be considered;
- financial and technological resources available to the undertaking;
- the access which the undertaking has to raw materials and outlets; ie if the undertaking controls its sources of supply and its distribution outlets it is likely to be more competitive and more dominant;
- the behaviour of the undertaking.

Having established that the undertaking has a dominant position in the market, it must then be decided whether that position has in fact been abused.

Article 86 itself gives several examples of abuse of a dominant position. This list is not intended to be exhaustive. Before looking at some cases demonstrating the kinds of restriction which have been held to amount to abuse, the final requirement is that the abuse must affect trade between member states. Establishing this is not perhaps as difficult as one might imagine. In *British Leyland plc* v *EC Commission* (1984) the European Court held that it was not necessary to establish any *specific* effect so long as there was evidence that the abuse *might* affect trade between member states.

4. Case examples

The following cases illustrate the kinds of restriction which are subject to attack under Article 86.

Hilti AG v *EC Commission* (1985): Hilti were manufacturers of nail guns. They attempted to tie sales of their cartridge magazines to sales of their nails by applying a range of pressures and sanctions to customers and importers, including discounts and litigation. This was found to be an abuse of a dominant position, evidenced by Hilti's ability to act independently without regard to its customers or other competitors.

United Brands Co and United Brands Continentaal BV v *EC Commission* (1976): United Brands were producers of bananas. They owned plantations, refrigerated vessels and warehouses all over Europe. They tried to impose conditions on importers to prevent them re-selling the bananas while they were still green. They also had different price tariffs for different countries within the Common Market. They were held to be in a dominant position. There were no acceptable substitutes for the bananas in certain sections of the Community, and United Brands were therefore held to be abusing their dominant position. It is interesting to note that the court was not swayed by the argument that the consumer would be getting a better, more standardised product if it allowed the restrictions to be imposed because it would mean that only those with the right storage and ripening facilities would be able to sell them.

Hoffman-La Roche & Co AG v *EC Commission* (1976): A pharmaceutical company had a dominant position in the vitamin market. It required its customers to undertake to buy all or most of their requirements from them, offering them as a reward what were termed "fidelity rebates" which were, in effect, discounts. There were also clauses in its agreements with its customers which provided that the customers could ask the company to lower its prices if they found other competitors selling at lower prices. It was held that all these clauses were in breach of Article 86. The customers' freedom to buy from competitors was restricted and the company could effectively cut out potential rivals by lowering its prices.

The Union de Remorquage Case: Three tug companies in Antwerp had formed a cartel which had a complete monopoly of the business. Another company, SSB, was formed in 1963 to begin operations in 1964. In anticipation of this, the tug companies began introducing new terms to ship owners offering them substantial discounts if they would enter into exclusive contracts with the cartel companies. It was significant that, had the ship owners used SSB instead of the cartel companies, the ship owners would have sustained a financial loss. The court therefore held the practice of the cartel companies to be an abuse of a dominant position.

The Brinkhof Case: Seven out of eight forwarding agents for cut flowers in Holland formed themselves into a co-operative which was able to negotiate substantial reductions with the Dutch Railways. Brinkhof was the eighth company. The Dutch Railways also offered Brinkhof the same reductions but, because Brinkhof obtained some business formerly held by the co-operative, they withdrew the reductions from Brinkhof when the contract expired. It was held that the Railways could not give to Brinkhof different terms from those they were offering to the co-operative companies.

The GEMA Case: GEMA was a society of composers, authors and publishers in Germany, formed for copyright protection purposes – the only one of its kind in that country. It was a condition of membership that each member had to assign all his existing and future rights for all countries to GEMA for at least six years and GEMA had the right to exploit these rights. GEMA then distributed royalties according to a "classification procedure". GEMA was held to be in abuse of its dominant position within Germany. It was also held to be abusing its position because its licensing contracts with the record manufacturers required them to pay a full royalty, even where a record included non-protected works, and included other similarly stringent royalty conditions.

It is clear, therefore, that Article 86 has a wide scope indeed –

wider perhaps than is often imagined by non-specialists in competition law. It is certainly wider than the restraint doctrine, but from the examples above it can be seen that it also includes restrictions which would have been likely to fall within the ambit of the restraint doctrine.

The relationship between Article 85 and Article 86 is that the former is concerned mainly with the anti-competitive effects of independent organisations grouping together. Article 86 is aimed more at independent undertakings and the danger that they will abuse their market power. Although there may be an overlap, the Articles are intended together to cover the range of anti-competitive practices. It is possible for a particular restriction to be in breach of both Article 85 and Article 86.

The Commission is given wide powers under Regulation 17 (see Chapter 7) to deal with any suspected breach of Article 86. It can *inter alia* make sector inquiries, looking at competition in the whole of a particular market sector to identify abuses which distort competition, and can undertake on-the-spot investigations. It can request all necessary information, examine books and records, enter premises, take copies of documents and conduct oral examinations. In *Hoechst AG* v *EC Commission* (1988) the legality of a "dawn raid" was upheld. The Commission may also request the relevant authorities in the member state itself to undertake the investigation on its behalf.

Having identified an abuse, the Commission has considerable authority to impose fines and take other measures to prevent the abuse, although the parties have a right to a hearing before the Commission takes any action. Persons having a "sufficient interest" in the matter are also entitled to be heard.

Clearly there are no exemptions under Article 86 but the Commission has power to give a "negative clearance" in respect of a proposed action (Article 2). An agreement may be notified to the Commission and a comfort letter may be issued.

5. Article 86 and the English courts

As regards the position of the English courts in upholding Article 86, Article 9(3) of Regulation 17 provides that so long as the Commission has not initiated a negative clearance, investigation or exemption procedure, the authorities in member states are competent to apply Articles 85 and 86. An English court may therefore find that an agreement is in breach of Article 85 or Article

86 and declare it void. It cannot, however, fine the defaulting undertaking. The court may grant an injunction, as occurred in *Cutsforth* v *Mansfield Inns Ltd* (1986). In that case, the defendant brewery company had taken over a number of tied houses in a particular area. The plaintiffs were suppliers of pin tables and gaming machines in the area. The tenancy agreements for the tied houses provided that the pin tables and gaming machines installed by the tenants must be supplied by persons on an approved list. The plaintiffs' name was not on the list, although the public houses in question had previously been among their customers. They made a complaint to the Commission and at the same time applied for an interlocutory injunction. The injunction was granted on the basis that there was a case to answer of infringement of the Treaty.

Apparently, the court can also make a declaration. The question of whether or not damages can be awarded was considered by the House of Lords in *Garden Cottage Foods Ltd* v *Milk Marketing Board* (1983). In that case, a company, which was owned and managed by Mr and Mrs Bunch, carried on the business of buying and reselling bulk butter. The company bought 90 per cent of its bulk butter from the Milk Marketing Board between May 1980 and April 1982 and sold most of it on to a Dutch customer. In March 1982, the Board informed the company that it had decided to limit the sale of bulk butter to four other distributors in England and Wales followng a review of its sales and market strategy. The company would therefore have no alternative but to try and buy its butter from the other distributors. The company issued proceedings in the English courts, for breach of Article 86 claiming an injunction. The case reached the House of Lords where it had to be decided whether it was possible for the court to award damages in respect of a breach of Article 86 and, if so, whether that would in any event be a satisfactory remedy. They decided that an individual citizen of the United Kingdom who has been affected by an infringement of Article 86 is entitled to an award of damages, and therefore the usual conditions apply in determining whether damages are in the circumstances a sufficient remedy and whether, on the balance of convenience, an interlocutory injunction should or should not be granted.

This case and the *Cutsforth* case highlight the fact that action can be taken by an individual who is either a party to the agreement or whose interests have been affected by it.

It is clear, therefore, that Articles 85 and 86 go a long way further than does the restraint doctrine in controlling anti-competitive provisions in agreements. They also provide a better selection of remedies and even allow a stranger to an agreement to obtain redress where his interests have been damaged by it. It seems that the English courts are prepared to grant an interlocutory injunction in cases which are urgent and as explained elsewhere in this book, an interlocutory injunction, despite its temporary nature, will have the practical effect of deciding which of the parties is to succeed.

The legal adviser must therefore tread warily.

6. Conclusions

Like the preceding chapter, this does not purport to be a comprehensive summary of European competition law. By way of conclusion, some points are suggested which may sound warning bells for the draftsman, in which case he is advised to undertake further research before drafting the agreement.

Article 86 may apply where:

- one of the undertakings has a dominant position in a specific market in the United Kingdom or part of it, or in any wider geographical area; or
- the agreement will give one or more undertakings a dominant position in such a market; and
- the agreement contains restrictions which, amongst others, could have the effect of:
  - tying a party to buy from a particular supplier;
  - unfair prices being charged or resale prices being restricted;
  - allowing a supplier to refuse to supply;
  - applying discriminatory terms as between equivalent trading parties;
  - imposing supplementary obligations which have no connection with the subject-matter of the contract;
  - imposing unfair trading conditions; and
- there is a *potential* effect on inter-member trade (but this does not mean that an agreement between undertakings in the same member state may not be caught if the restrictions discourage one party from trading in another member state).

An individual can be an "undertaking" for the purposes of either Article 85 or Article 86, so agreements between individuals are not exempt. Moreover, the "affects inter-member trade" requirement cannot always be relied on to exempt the agreement because restriction can affect inter-member trade simply by in some way (impliedly or expressly) discouraging a party from trading in another member state — there is no need to prove that he has ever traded in Europe or that he has any intention of doing so (see the *Pronuptia* case, Chapter 7). A far wider range of agreements is potentially caught than is often imagined, and it is advisable to make quite sure that the agreement in question is not one of them.

Chapter 9

Advising about restraints

A covenant in restraint of trade is usually only a very small provision in a much larger contract and, as such, can very easily be overlooked when time is of the essence and attention is focused on what at the time are considered to be the more important central issues. It is therefore neither unusual nor surprising to find a standard precedent being drafted wholesale into a contract, sometimes without prior consultation with the client and with no more than the briefest explanation to the client as to the purpose and effect of the clause.

The case of *DW Moore & Co* v *Ferrier* (1988) focused attention on the drafting of this seemingly unimportant part of a contract and sounded a warning for any draftsman who might consider that less care need be taken over it than over other clauses. The defendants in this case were solicitors and their plaintiff clients were insurance brokers. The defendants were instructed by the plaintiffs to draw up agreements concerning the employment and issue of shares to F, a director in the plaintiff company. The plaintiffs claimed to have instructed the defendants *inter alia* to draft a covenant in restraint to prevent F from setting up in competition if he left the company. The restraint which was included in the agreement was worded as follows:

> "the parties hereto mutually agree further that in the event of any of the parties hereto ceasing to be a member of the Company such person shall not engage in any other business connected with insurance or insurance broking in any way whatever within a radius of fifteen miles of King's Lynn for a period of three years from the date of such person ceasing to be a member of the Company and in particular

but without prejudice to the generality of the foregoing shall not canvass the Company's clients or trade connection in any way whatever."

According to the statement of claim, the plaintiffs were concerned about the adequacy of the clause and were told by the defendants that the covenant was "a valid and binding covenant" and sufficient in law to prevent F from engaging "for a period of three years from the date of his ceasing to be a director of and/or employed" by the plaintiff company in the business of insurance broking within the restricted area.

F subsequently resigned as director and employee of the company and set up on his own account as an insurance broker within the restricted area. On seeking to enforce the covenant, the plaintiffs discovered that, contrary to what the defendants had told them, it was effective only if F ceased to be a member, ie a shareholder in the company; since he had not given up his shares, the covenant did not protect them. They sued the defendants in negligence.

The appeal was on the preliminary issue of whether the claim was statute-barred. The Court of Appeal found that the plaintiffs' cause of action arose when the agreement was signed and that the claim was statute-barred. The negligence claim itself was therefore untried and it must be stressed that the truth or otherwise of the plaintiff's statement of claim was never assessed, nor do we know what defence the defendants might have had, and the substance of the claim must be treated as hypothetical for our purposes. However, it is clear from the judgments that, if what the plaintiffs alleged were true, there would have been a cause of action. At first instance the judge, Robin Stewart QC, found that the plaintiffs had sought a particular form of protection and, on the face of it, it appeared they had not obtained it. The important point was that the value of the contract was less without that protection than it would have been with it and they had therefore suffered quantifiable damage.

On appeal, the judges agreed with him. Neill LJ particularly made the point that the benefit of a restrictive covenant can be sold and is therefore of value, especially in relation to the business in question where personal contact was of the utmost importance. That value was so self-evident that it did not need to be specially proved.

It seems, therefore, that the negligent drafting of a covenant in restraint of trade, at least in this type of case, will automatically injure the client, whether the agreement in question is a business sale or an employment contract, because the value of the client's business will be less than if he had a covenant which, as he believes, is enforceable. The implication of this for legal draftsmen is quite far-reaching.

Assuming that the plaintiffs could prove their case as it appeared on the pleadings, the court was confident that they would have an action either in contract or in tort, and the fact that damages might be difficult to assess would not be any bar, since they had quite clearly suffered injury to the value of their business.

The point which seems clear from all the judgments is that, whatever defences the defendants might have raised on trial of the substantive issue in this particular case, as a general principle, negligent advice and drafting in respect of a restrictive covenant is to be considered no differently from any other form of negligence and it is of no use to argue that any restrictive covenant might be struck down by the court or that the plaintiffs suffered no real damage.

The problem raised by *Moore* v *Ferrier*, so far as practitioners are concerned, is that it alerts clients to a potential cause of action. It is possible that in future cases where a restrictive covenant is found to be unenforceable as a result of the restraint doctrine, clients may be more inclined to turn to their solicitors and claim that their loss was the fault of the solicitors for not advising them properly or not drafting a covenant which protected them. How should a practitioner protect himself against such a claim? What must he do to be able to show that he has acted with sufficient care and skill to discharge his duty to the client? It is submitted that he must be able to show that he advised the client fully concerning the interests which could be protected and as to what might and might not be considered reasonable protection, took a great deal of care in taking instructions, and drafted a covenant which was carefully tailored to provide the maximum possible protection for the client's interests. Anything less might well leave a legal adviser open to a claim for damages for breach of contract or negligence. On this basis, it is believed that anyone who merely inserts a standard precedent without careful consideration, or simply warns the client that any covenant may fall foul of the doctrine so that it does not really matter what form the covenant takes, is failing to achieve the proper standard of care applicable to the situation.

Clearly the nature of the advice and instructions will depend very much on the type of contract being drafted and the party for whom the solicitor is acting. Every instance will be different. Experienced practitioners will have their own procedures and techniques which may not always accord with the author's. What follows is therefore a subjective review of steps to be taken and points to be borne in mind which has, nevertheless, been compiled after careful reading of many of the cases on restraint of trade.

In this chapter, it is intended to deal with taking instructions from and giving advice to the client. The next chapter will concentrate on the actual drafting of the clause.

1. Business sale agreements

(a) Advising the purchaser

With this type of agreement, the draftsman will naturally have taken careful instructions on the exact nature of the business and what precisely is to be included in the sale. The client should be advised of the need to insert restraints into the agreement and warned of the very real danger that the vendor may set up in competition close by, which of course he will be able to do in the absence of any contractual restraint.

Having been advised of this, the client is likely to want the greatest possible restrictions to be placed on the vendor's post-sale activities. It will therefore be necessary to advise him that protection can be achieved only for the business being purchased, not for any other business in which the purchaser is involved, and only for a reasonable duration within a reasonable geographical area. The client must be informed that the only thing capable of protection is the goodwill purchased, ie the name and customer connection, and although that may include future as well as existing customers of the business, it does not include the future possibility of the business expanding into new areas.

Although the purchaser may be protected by the general law on breach of confidence so far as confidential information and secret processes which are involved in the sale are concerned, if there are trade secrets involved in the sale, the client should be advised to take a reasonably drawn covenant which will protect him against use or disclosure by the vendor. Whether this should be extended to protect the purchaser against potential danger from the vendor going to work for the rival is a matter for discussion, but the client should be advised that he can obtain only limited protection in this regard.

As regards customer connection, there will often be an agreed list of customers which will give a clue to the extent of the business in geographical terms. The agreed list might also form the basis of a non-solicitation or a non-dealing covenant. The duration, if it is agreed between the parties, should prove to be no particular stumbling block and, if necessary, the vendor could be subject to a reasonable restriction for the rest of his life if the purchaser has good reason to fear damage to his goodwill, for example because the vendor's name is very well known.

(b) Advising the vendor

It will of course be up to the purchaser initially to draw up the restraint clauses in the agreement, and these should be examined very carefully and discussed with the vendor. The vendor may well be indignant at the thought that the agreement might restrict his future activities. It is up to his legal adviser to explain to him the necessity of protection from the purchaser's point of view, together with the fact that any purchaser of his business will be likely to require some form of restraint and that he is unlikely to get a sale without it.

A dilemma is posed by the purchaser who inserts a restraint which is clearly very wide. Does one simply accept the covenant on the ground that the courts will refuse to enforce it as unreasonable, or should one negotiate a more reasonable covenant which is likely to be enforced against the client? Much depends on the actual wording, and cases like *Littlewoods Organisation* v *Harris* and *Goldsoll* v *Goldman* should be consulted (see Chapters 1, 2 and 6) to ascertain whether this may be a case in which the court is able or likely to validate the covenant by reading in limiting words or by severance, and it should be remembered that the courts have accepted some very wide covenants in connection with business sales. The potential uncertainty of a wide covenant, therefore, needs to be balanced against the risk of a narrower covenant which might not impede the client in his future plans at all. The author has known of cases where simply challenging a covenant on the grounds that it is unreasonably restrictive has led to the withdrawal of the covenant altogether, and this, too, may be worth a try!

If the covenant is to be challenged at all, the aim of the solicitor acting for the vendor is to ensure that the covenant does not impede the vendor in what he may reasonably wish to do following the sale. Obviously, therefore, the covenant cannot be considered properly without taking instructions and some thought being given to what the vendor intends to do. He may intend to retire from active employment, in which case a covenant restraining him from taking any active part in business would be acceptable, but it should not be so wide as to prevent him investing in another business as, say, a sleeping partner or shareholder, or helping out a member of the family in a legitimate business venture. The vendor, too, having been in business all his life, may find retirement tedious and the covenant ought not to be so wide that it prevents him going back to work if he wishes to do so, as long as his coming out of retirement does not bring him into unfair competition with the purchaser.

The vendor who intends to set up in business elsewhere needs to be advised with particular care. If there is a strong possibility that some of his customers will follow him whatever he does, a non-solicitation covenant needs to be examined very closely. It may be necessary to clarify exactly what amounts to solicitation. If the restrictions also cover "dealing", this should be brought to the client's attention as he may unwittingly find himself in breach of the restriction. The vendor may have decided that he is tired of being his own boss and may have accepted employment with another. Again, the vendor should be advised that, if this is the case, he should not accept any restriction which might prevent him taking up such employment.

Any geographical area or duration must also be discussed in the context of what the vendor wishes to do with his life. If he is to accept a lifelong restraint, for example, he must be sure that he has no intention of going back into the trade at all and that he is not merely taking a sabbatical. A geographical restraint may mean that the vendor will have to move away, perhaps from an area in which he and his family have become firmly established, if he wishes to continue in business. This ought to be pointed out to him as it may not have been fully realised, and if a country-wide restraint is justified, he may even have to go abroad. If he thinks he can set up in business or be employed just outside the restricted area, which may be quite small, the restrictions should be examined to see if they include dealing with any former customers inside the restricted area and, if so, the vendor should be informed so as not, again, to be unknowingly in breach.

All in all, it is submitted, properly advising the vendor client does not mean simply drawing his attention to any restrictions in the agreement and asking if he is prepared to accept them. He is unlikely to have the solicitor's expertise in foreseeing possible future situations and in ascertaining whether they fall within the ambit of a restriction. A good legal adviser should therefore explain to the client the full implications of the clause, asking questions and making suggestions aimed at directing the client's attention to precisely the extent to which the restrictions will interfere with his future plans. After a full discussion with the client, it may be necessary to try to negotiate alternative wording which allows him the freedom he wishes without interfering unduly with the purchaser's business.

2. Directors' service contracts

(a) Advising the company

A unique and interesting aspect of service contracts is that where instructions come for drafting the first directors' service contracts for a company, they will usually come from the very people who are to be the other parties, ie the directors themselves. The board of a company may decide to award itself service contracts for a variety of reasons, and clauses often include provisions relating to entrenchment, enshrinement of rights to, for example, remuneration and the method by which it is to be calculated, entitlement to holidays and pensions etc, and the division of specific duties between them. The legal adviser will not be expected to take the harder line he would normally take on behalf of a covenantee, and it may be that no restraints are required. In essence, where the directors are all the members of the company, this situation is very much more like drawing up a partnership agreement than a contract of employment, and fairness may be the overriding principle.

However, as explained in Chapter 4, much of the modern litigation has centred not on interpretation of express restraint clauses but on breach of other duties, particularly fiduciary duties. Many company directors are surprisingly ignorant of company law, and a legal adviser would probably be failing in his duty if he did not ascertain whether his clients possess such knowledge; if his clients do not possess such knowledge, he should explain that although no express restrictions are to be incorporated into the service agreement, there are many things a director may be restrained from doing, either because it would be a breach of his duties as a director or because he would be breaking his duty of fidelity as an employee, or because it might amount to a breach of confidence.

The contract to be drafted may, however, be a "one-off" for a managing or other executive director who has just been appointed or has recently joined the board. Here it is quite clear that the adviser is acting for the company and that the director must look after his own interests by seeking independent legal advice.

Although the same considerations as to common law breach of duty etc will apply, the company should be advised to have express restrictions incorporated into the contract.

It is advisable to have in the contract not only post-termination restrictions but also clear restrictions on setting up in competition, disclosing information etc during the subsistence of the contract of service. Although the director is likely to be, purely by virtue of his position on the board, in possession of confidential information about the company, it is clear that this may not be sufficient to prevent him from setting up his own business in competition either during or after termination of his employment, and it may be a moot point whether the director is using the company's confidential information or his own skill and knowledge. However, although it may be possible to obtain slightly more from a restrictive covenant post-termination, the director may usually only be restrained from using specific information which is capable of being carried away in his head and which he knows to be confidential information amounting to a trade secret. Perhaps the best advice for the company is to try and ensure that the information which it wishes to protect has the necessary quality of confidentiality about it: is highly restricted in its distribution, is specifically marked "highly confidential" and acknowledged by the director to be so.

Directors setting up their own businesses, or moving to rival companies, often take other key employees with them. This does not amount to a breach of duty, but it can be argued that an express covenant against this is not in restraint of trade and is therefore advisable. However, it is a good idea for the company to cover the situation in "belt and braces" fashion by ensuring that the employees themselves are subject to restrictions on termination.

Managing directors and other important executives of large companies are subject to the modern danger of being "head-hunted" by a rival concern. In the absence of a non-competition covenant, there is nothing to prevent this. Such a covenant is therefore advisable, but needs to be very carefully drafted so as not to give the appearance of being a covenant purely aimed at stifling competition. It will be upheld only if the director or executive in question has strong customer connections or is possessed of confidential information amounting to a trade secret, but there are signs that the situation itself may lead the court to take a more lenient view of such a clause. The clause ought to be carefully restricted in terms of the actual business of the company and the geographical and temporal limits. If the executive is concerned with only one facet of the company's business interests, the restraint should be limited to that category of business. The company ought to be warned that, even if carefully drawn, the clause may not succeed in providing it with the protection it hopes for, but is worth the attempt as it will not be protected otherwise. It may be possible to restrict the clause to a particular trade rival or rivals.

Where the director is an employee, rather than treated as a member of the company, the courts may take a stricter view of restraints than they would take with other kinds of agreement. The company should be advised of this and the possibility that however carefully the restrictions are drafted, they may still fail. However, so far as being an employee is concerned, it at least means that during his employment the director is subject to restraints on the ground of fidelity. He is also bound by strong fiduciary duties as a director, and if he obtains any lucrative business opportunity through his position in the company, he may have to account to the company for the proceeds. These duties may possibly be built on in the contract and their extent clarified. The duties may in some circumstances continue after termination of the contract, and it may be worth considering how far this may give scope for protection. The company will not, however, be able to rely on post-termination restrictions if the director is unfairly or wrongfully dismissed.

Finally, the company may be advised that post-termination restrictions on solicitation are likely to be upheld. It should be remembered that the restriction ought not to extend to customers who were not customers during the period of the director's employment with the company, but that even though the customer may have already made it clear that he no longer wishes to do business with the company, the non-solicitation covenant may still be upheld against the former director as regards that customer. This is in contrast to the common law position where a director who sets up a competing business after leaving the company is not prevented from servicing a former customer of the company.

(b) Advising the director

The director is likely to seek advice about the contract when it is made, although he may of course not do so until he intends leaving the company and wishes to know the extent of the restrictions. At the earlier stage, when he will naturally be committed to working for the company, he may have some difficulty foreseeing what might happen if he should become disillusioned with the company or if the company should wish to dispense with his services at a later date. At that stage, too, he will be more inclined to accept restrictions on his future conduct, however unreasonable they might appear to him later.

Notwithstanding *Balston* v *Headline Filters*, which was in any case concerned mainly with fiduciary duties, it is probably true to say that a director is considerably more restricted than other employees in what he can do after termination of his contract. He may also find that, if he holds shares in the company, he may be subjected to restrictions in a shareholders' agreement or contract of sale, and these are likely to be interpreted more liberally than those in his contract of service (see below). A solicitor ought to make his client aware of all this, so that at least he is forewarned. As a general rule, it is helpful to advise a newly appointed director of his common law duties, unless he already knows them, and he may be advised as to the extent to which any express clauses in his contract of service elaborate and amplify such duties.

If the express restrictions in the service agreement appear to be unreasonably wide, as explained above in connection with business sale agreements, the solicitor will be faced with the dilemma of advising whether to permit them to remain as they are in the hope that the court will refuse to enforce them, or whether to negotiate narrower restrictions. Although the court may be inclined to take a less liberal view of restraints in what is essentially a contract of employment, the solicitor needs to consider whether the court could, if it wished, validate the clause by either deleting words or reading in words of limitation. There are probably very few wide clauses to which this approach could not be taken if the court were so minded, and the legal adviser should be particularly wary of clauses aimed at permitting the court to interpret the clause in the way which seems most reasonable to it. The client ought to be made aware of the difficulty involved.

If the company's business extends to the whole of the United Kingdom, or to other parts of the world as well, the director should be advised that he could be in deep difficulties in finding other employment after leaving the employment of the company if his contract includes a non-competition covenant. Efforts might best then be aimed at negotiating a clause which is more limited in scope, for example a non-solicitation clause or a clause limited to employment with particular rivals in the business. Should the company's business be more localised, the director might be well advised to bear in mind any plans which the company may have for expansion, for example by taking over rivals in other localities or setting up new plants.

As a general rule it is unwise to accept restraints unlimited in geographical area or duration. Although such a covenant might ultimately be struck down as unreasonable, the director, after termination of his employment, will find the future uncertain and may be forced to litigation to establish his right to work in a particular area. The threat of such litigation might well be sufficient to lock him into his contract with the company with little power to negotiate improved pay or conditions or to resist changes to his contract.

3. Contracts of employment

(a) Advising the company

Contracts of employment, rather more than directors' service contracts, are likely to be required in a standard form. The problem here is that the company may have a number of different kinds of employee who are to be covered by the same form of contract: secretarial and clerical staff in the offices, skilled and unskilled workers on the shop floor, for example. Certainly not all of them will be privy to confidential information or secret processes, or will have contact with customers. As far as duties, pay and conditions are concerned, the company may be left to insert the relevant details as necessary, but drafting a restraint clause is really a job for the legally qualified. The courts have occasionally been scornful of attempts to impose a standard form of restraint universally on employees and, although the modern view may be more liberal, it is still the case that where a standard form of contract is involved the courts are likely to be even more vigilant. Added to this is the problem that a clause which is to cover different types of employee is likely of necessity to be general in nature, which makes it easier for the court to strike it down. It ought therefore to be explained to the client that although a clause may protect him in respect of some employees, for example those who have a strong customer connection or are in possession of trade secrets, he cannot expect to receive protection from post-termination competition from all his employees. A clause which goes further than necessary to protect the employer *in respect of the particular employee in question* is void and unless the doctrine of severance applies or the court is willing or able to read in limiting words, the restriction will fail altogether, albeit that the ex-employee may have actually damaged the employer's reasonable interests.

During the course of the employment, the employer will of course be able to rely on the duty of fidelity which his employees owe to him, which may protect him against their working for a competitor (although this may not always be the case). The duty of confidence will continue after termination, of course, but following *Faccenda Chicken* v *Fowler* it is thought that an express post-termination covenant is advisable where the employee has confidential information which the employer does not want him to use or disclose to others. The employer's fears that such an employee may go into the service of a rival may well be justified. It does, after all, seem odd that employees are restrained from working for rival concerns while they are employed because they have confidential information (which does not necessarily amount to a trade secret) but not afterwards unless the information can actually be shown to amount to a trade secret. Given the extreme difficulty of distinguishing between information which is a trade secret and that which is not, the employer is well advised to try and increase the odds in his favour during the employment by ensuring that:

(i)   when the confidential information is divulged to an employee, he is made aware that the employer believes it to be confidential, for example documents containing confidential information might be clearly marked as such and information concerning processes etc should not be displayed in places where anyone who enters the workplace can read them;

(ii) information which the employer wishes to be kept secret from rivals is given a very restricted circulation within the company itself (the "need to know" principle, as it is called in the civil service);

(iii) where employees habitually handle confidential information, care should be taken that they do not take it for granted and the confidential nature of their employment should be impressed upon them.

As with other agreements, instructions will be needed as to the precise nature of the employer's business, its customers and the extent of its operation. Companies should be advised that, as with director-employees, any wrongful or unfair dismissal will release the employee from the restrictions in his contract. It may not, however, relieve him of his duty of confidentiality.

(b) Advising an employee

It is rare for the average employee to take advice concerning a contract of employment when he signs it. Usually, the question of restrictions will arise only when the employer alleges he has broken them. A new employer may seek advice from his solicitor as to whether someone he intends to employ is banned by restrictions in his contract with his former or current employer. Advice to an employee may be on much the same lines as that to a director, ie advice on his common law duties and the extent to which the contract seeks to expand on them. As to post-termination restrictions, he should be advised that their effectiveness will depend on the nature of his employment, whether he is to be entrusted with confidential information or have influential contact with customers. Whether he is or is not to be the recipient of confidential information or have customer contact is not, of course, his to decide. The position may, of course, change if he remains with the company for some time and is offered promotion. It can be argued that the employer need only disclose one important trade secret to an employee to have him bound by the restriction. There is very little that one can do for an employee because he will usually be in a weak negotiating position and the employer may not be inclined to make any changes to the contract, particularly if it is in standard form. The employee should, however, be made aware of the extent to which he could be restricted in the future if the restrictions were to be deemed reasonable and how he, like a director, might become locked into a contract with unsatisfactory pay and conditions.

4. Partnership agreements

A partnership agreement, it is to be remembered, is a kind of half-way house between contracts of employment and business sale agreements. The agreement essentially concerns the goodwill of the business and it is with this aspect that any restrictions are likely to be concerned.

The partners themselves may not have thought about what is to happen after the partnership is dissolved or when a partner dies. Although a partner is very restricted by his common law duty of good faith to the other partners in what he may do in terms of carrying on other businesses while he is still a partner, after he leaves the partnership the common law restricts him hardly at all and, like the unrestricted vendor of a business, he can set up next door as long as he does not represent himself as carrying on the old business or openly solicit its customers. It is therefore advisable to have some post-termination restrictions.

A legal adviser will normally be acting on behalf of all the partners when he draws up the initial agreement. Incoming partners are unlikely to have the power to re-negotiate restraint covenants, since it will be argued that if all the other partners are prepared to accept such restraints then it is only fair that the incoming partner should do so.

Fairness, or mutuality, in fact, is the key factor in relation to dealing with restraints accepted by partners and, so long as it operates fairly as between the partners, a well-drafted clause will generally be upheld because the partners are usually on an equal footing in negotiations and in a far better position to negotiate terms than employees. In addition, there will be consideration – in the form of goodwill – passing under the agreement. Fairness seems to mean that all partners should be subject to the same restriction, rather than that the restriction should be proportionate to the number of clients serviced by individual partners, although there are dicta to suggest otherwise.

As all partners have the right to be involved in management, to full disclosure of partnership affairs and to make contracts on behalf of the partnership, it is likely that they will have access both to customers and to trade secrets, if any. All the partners will be known to customers by name, even if only because their names appear on the notepaper, and usually the connection will be stronger than that. All the partners have an interest in the goodwill.

The advice stage is therefore a matter of taking instructions from the clients as to the extent of the business and getting them to agree on a reasonable geographical extent and duration. A non-solicitation covenant should always be included. Whether there is need for an anti-competitive covenant will depend on the particular circumstances of the case. However if, for example, a partner's name appears as part of the firm's name, it might be wise, in order to avoid confusion, to restrain him from setting up under his own name after retirement, although there is some doubt as to whether a provision such as this will be upheld.

Another question is whether a covenant should operate on dissolution or only on retirement. On dissolution, of course, there will be no goodwill left to protect and it would be difficult, if not impossible, to justify such a covenant as reasonable, even if taken by all the partners.

A final point is whether a partner is to be allowed to operate as a consultant or not after leaving the firm. Provided that the consultancy is something different and in the nature of a "higher authority", for example he will not be acting direct for clients but will be receiving his clientele second-hand through others in the profession, there is probably no reason why he should be restrained and probably no justification for doing so. A covenant should therefore be drafted so as to make it clear that he is not prohibited from acting in this way; otherwise it may be considered to be too extensive and, consequently, void.

5. Tying agreements

Tying agreements are usually drafted on behalf of large organisations by lawyers who are skilled in the drafting of this type of agreement. It is therefore not to them but to a solicitor who may be consulted by the other party to such an agreement that this section is directed.

These agreements will usually be in the standard form which is best suited to the covenantee's business operations. The covenantee is therefore unlikely to be enthusiastic about negotiating any of the terms in the agreement. If under, or ancillary to, the agreement, the client contracts to invest a substantial sum of money, or if the agreement ties him to purchase at not inconsiderable cost goods, services, know-how etc from the other party, he should be counselled to think very carefully about the whole deal, including any restrictions involved, and in particular the duration of any restraints.

When considering the restrictions in the agreement in question, it is worth noting the following points:

- Is the agreement for a fixed period of more than five years?
- Is there provision for the covenantor to terminate the agreement before the end of the term?
- If there is a provision for termination by the covenantor, are there any penalties for terminating before the agreement expires?
- If there is a provision for the covenantee to terminate before the expiry of the agreement, can he do so in such a way as to leave the covenantor in difficulties, for example because he cannot get supplies for his business or is subject to post-termination restrictions on competition?
- Do the ties in the agreement concern only the main product or service which is the subject matter of the agreement, or is the covenantor tied in respect of any ancillary products or services?

- If there are any royalties payable for know-how, or for use of trade marks, are they reasonable in the context of the agreement as a whole?
- Is there any way in which the covenantor is empowered to fix or restrict resale prices?
- Are there any post-termination restrictions on the covenantor and, if so, are their duration and extent reasonable in the context of the agreement as a whole?
- If there are any restrictions on the use of any know-how provided under the agreement, including post-termination restrictions, are they reasonable in the context of the information which will be made available to the covenantee by the covenantor?
- Is the covenantor allotted a particular territory and is he permitted to trade outside that territory?

6. Agreements ancillary to employment

The case law relating to agreements which the employee may enter into as a consequence of his employment was discussed fully in Chapter 3. These agreements include pension arrangements and shareholders' or share sale agreements.

The basic rule is that anti-competition post-termination restrictions which are extracted in consideration for the granting or for the paying of a pension are probably to be treated as a means of obtaining an employer-employee covenant and are likely to be void. However, the new approach to employment contracts, which appears to be emerging from the Court of Appeal, may mean that the rule cannot be relied on as firmly as it has been in the past.

Where the restrictions are contained in a shareholders' or share sale agreement, the employee-shareholder, however small his holding, is likely to be treated as part-owner of the goodwill, and the court will construe the restrictions more generously. Thus, any restrictions in this kind of agreement should be examined very carefully if the adviser is acting on behalf of the employee.

Chapter 10

Drafting a restraint clause

A restraint clause is, of course, only a small part of the agreement. Nevertheless, if the job is to be done properly some special thought must be given to its drafting. Naturally, the clause will be drafted in the context of the agreement as a whole and so it is only possible to give some general guidelines here. First of all there are a few general points, arising from the many decisions concerning restraint clauses, which may be borne in mind when attempting to draft a valid restraint.

1. General drafting points

(a) Ambiguity

Given the fact that there can be no guarantees as to what will be acceptable, it may be tempting to draft restraint clauses which can be read in more than one way in the hope that the court will construe them as favourably as possible. Unfortunately, there is no guarantee that the court will take a favourable view. In addition, ambiguity or vagueness makes it very difficult for the parties themselves to know what the limits of the restrictions are, and expensive litigation over the meaning of the restraints becomes a strong likelihood. Clarity is therefore definitely something which should be aimed for whatever the type of agreement.

(b) General words

As indicated in Chapter 6, there has recently been a tendency to read in limiting words where the draftsman has used general phraseology which, without limiting words, would be deemed too wide. However, as explained, there is certainly no unanimity among the judiciary as to when (or indeed if) it is possible to read in words, and the extent to which the courts are prepared to do so. It is therefore better practice for the draftsman to establish and insert the requisite limitations rather than leaving it to chance. For example, a restriction from selling "any goods similar to those sold by the company" may look reasonable at first sight but if the company has a number of ranges and if the covenantor happens only to be concerned with one of them, the phrase is likely to be judged far too wide. The use of words limiting the restriction to those goods with whose sale the covenantor was concerned is far more likely to be acceptable to the court and, at the same time, probably more closely reflects the intentions of the parties.

(c) Illustrative words

The *eiusdem generis* rule is usually applied to general words following or followed by particular examples, and may be applied rather more strictly here than in respect of other types of clause. For example, the phrase "as sole trader, partner, director or in any other capacity" may be interpreted so as to exclude "as shareholder" on the ground that shareholders are not necessarily concerned in the management of a company. Another danger with restraint clauses is that the courts may well construe a list of examples as exhaustive on the ground that the general words would be too wide otherwise.

(d) Definitions

In trying to produce restraints which are both clear and sufficiently limited so as to be reasonable, one can easily become tied up in a long, convoluted sentence. As a matter of good draftsmanship, it is better practice to keep the restraint itself as short and easy to read as possible, although one cannot always make it as short as one would like. One way is to use a definitions clause. For example, in dealing with the sale of a business, it is usual to define in some detail the business actually being sold and refer to it thereafter as "the business" or something similar. This will greatly assist the drafting of a restraint clause where (provided the business has been accurately described in the definitions clause) the protection can be seen by definition to be limited precisely to the interest meriting protection.

(e) Reference to other parts of the agreement

There is a strong probability that the court will look to the rest of the agreement in construing any restraints. The restraint clauses should therefore be drafted so as to tie in exactly with the rest of the agreement, using similar phraseology where appropriate so as to reflect clearly the parties' intentions as a whole. There certainly ought to be no ambiguity as between the restraint clauses and any other part of the agreement.

(f) Separate restrictive clauses

If a number of restrictions are involved, for example disclosing trade secrets, soliciting customers, and working for a rival firm, it is better drafting practice to have them in separate clauses or subclauses. Not only does this increase the clarity and simplicity of the agreement, but it also allows scope for the operation of the doctrine of severance. Each clause or subclause must, however, be drafted so that, if necessary, it could stand alone.

Example:

"For a period of one year from termination howsoever of his employment hereunder, the Employee:

(a) shall not solicit either directly or indirectly on his own account or on behalf of any other person the custom of any customer of the Employer who was the Employer's customer during the period of the Employee's employment hereunder;

(b) shall not sell or supply or deliver the restricted goods (as herein defined) to any customer of the Employer who was the Employer's customer during the period of the Employee's employment hereunder;

(c) shall not deal on his own account or on behalf of any other person with any customer of the Employer who was the Employer's customer during the period of the Employee's employment hereunder;

(d) shall not be engaged or concerned on his own account or as a partner shareholder or director or as an employee in any business selling the restricted goods (as herein defined) within a radius of five miles from the Employer's place of business."

A particular ploy often used by draftsmen is to draft a series of similar restraints ranked in order of severity with (perhaps) an invitation to the court to choose whichever it considers reasonable.

Example:

"The vendor agrees that he will not be engaged or concerned in any business selling the restricted goods (as herein defined) for a period of five years from the date of this agreement:

(a) within a radius of 15 miles from the principal place of business (as defined); or

(b) within a radius of 10 miles from the principal place of business (as defined); or

(c) within a radius of 5 miles from the principal place of business (as defined),

whichever the Court shall consider to be reasonable."

To the author's knowledge this has not been tested in the English courts. The closest to this was a clause which the Scottish courts had the opportunity of reviewing (see Chapter 6) in *Hinton & Higgs (UK) Ltd* v *Murphy and Valentine* (1989), which allowed the court to adjust the form of words by deletion in order to find a reasonable clause. This was upheld, although only a minor adjustment was necessary. It is submitted that the court ought to be prepared to strike out the unreasonable subclause(s) under the doctrine of restraint on the ground that the parties have agreed between themselves that they will abide by whichever version the court considers to be reasonable. Certainly, where all the court is being asked to do is to sever the unreasonable parts, this does not seem to be unreasonable. However, it does come dangerously close to asking the court to decide the agreement for the parties, and it leads to uncertainty between the parties as to what exact limits they have agreed, making it a virtual certainty that they will, unless they come to some agreement in the future, have to ask the court to decide in the long run.

(g) Consistency

If it is proposed to use more than one clause or subclause to describe the restrictions, particular attention must be paid to the consistency of the wording. If, for example, a word is used in one clause but left out of another, it is likely to be assumed that the omission from the second clause was deliberate and the sense of the second clause will therefore be deemed to be different. It is rarely assumed in this sort of case that if a word is used in one clause but omitted from another it was intended to be implied into the second clause.

Example:

"(a) the Employee shall not solicit the custom of a customer of the Employer (as defined) either on his own account or as a director, partner or shareholder in any other business;

(b) the Employee shall not be concerned in any business competing with the business of the Employer on his own account or as director or shareholder."

There is a strong likelihood that subclause (b) will be read as permitting the employee to compete in business as a partner since this word has been omitted.

The distinction in meaning between words like "use" and "disclose" in relation to confidential information has been admitted by the courts. Since one word does not necessarily overlap with the other, the omission of one of them will imply that that act is permitted.

(h) Alternatives

Particular care should be taken with the words "and" and "or", which may express alternatives or cumulatives. For example:

"the Employee shall be prohibited after the date of termination hereof from dealing with any customers of the Employer who were customers at the date of termination *and* from selling any products similar to those sold by the Employer".

The court has a choice whether to interpret the two restrictions as alternative (ie separate) or cumulative (ie both things must be taken together). If it chooses the former option, it may sever the second part if it considers it too wide and the first part to be reasonable. If on the other hand it prefers to consider the restrictions as cumulative, it may determine that the clause as a whole is too wide. If subclauses do have to be linked in this way, "or" is generally preferred to "and", where possible, as it allows more scope for severance to operate ("and" means that the court must decide whether the draftsman did in fact mean "or"). It is, however, even open to the judge to decide that where the word "or" is used the alternative means that the clause prohibited one or other of the actions but not both! This will not usually arise but it is safest wherever possible to use separate clauses for each restriction.

2. Particular types of covenant

In addition to general drafting considerations, there are special points to be considered which relate to the particular type of restraint or the particular type of agreement in question.

(a) Business sale agreements

It is to be remembered that although restraints in business sale agreements are perhaps to be interpreted more liberally in terms of duration and geographical area than other restraints, nevertheless in relation to the "business meriting protection" it seems that *British Reinforced Concrete Engineering Co Ltd* v *Schelff* (Chapter 2) still holds sway and the liberal approach to interpretation does not apply to this aspect. Great care should be taken, therefore, to ensure that the clause, in referring to the business to be protected, cannot be interpreted to cover more than what is actually being sold. For example if what is being sold is an antiquarian bookshop, a clause preventing the vendor from setting up in business as a "bookseller" might well be considered too wide, and the clause ought to be limited to "antiquarian" or "second-hand" books or some such phrase (a definition clause might also be needed).

(b) Non-solicitation covenants

In business sale agreements, these should be limited to customers who were customers of the business at the date of sale or within a reasonable time beforehand. What is reasonable will, of course, depend very much on the nature of the business and on the customer base. It may in some circumstances be reasonable to cover customers who have at any time been customers of the business, for example where the customer connection is very strong – as in a solicitor's business – or where dealings are lucrative but infrequent – as perhaps with an estate agency. The covenant should not be capable of interpretation so as to include customers of any part of the business which is not being sold.

In employment contracts, the clause should not usually cover customers with whom the employee had no connection, although it may be wise to include a restraint preventing him from memorising or copying lists of customers, or taking the lists away with him.

The words "previous or present" customers have usually been held to be too wide as they could include customers who ceased to be customers before the employee became employed by the employer. However, previous customers can be included if they were customers at any time during the employee's employment.

Generally speaking, the clause should be limited to customers who were customers during the period of the employee's employment but this may depend on the circumstances and the recurring nature of the particular business.

(c) Non-competition covenants

A general non-competition covenant will not usually be upheld, whatever the type of agreement. In other words, a non-competition covenant must be very clearly linked to an interest meriting protection.

In a business sale agreement this will be the business being sold, and from a drafting point of view this is fairly easy to deal with (see above).

In employment contracts, things are not quite so easy. From the draftsman's point of view, he is trying to draft a covenant which will protect the employer for many years ahead. Against him is the general antipathy of the court towards non-competition covenants. The first thing to consider is whether a non-solicitation covenant in conjunction, where necessary, with a prohibition on using or disclosing confidential information will do the job just as well, for this is far more likely to be upheld. If the employer does need wider protection from rivals, this must be very carefully drafted if it is to have any chance of succeeding. If confidential information is the basis of the need for protection, not only must the information be properly defined but the clause should also be limited to involvement in a competing business. If there are only certain major rivals in the business it may be worth specifying them by name (as was done in *Littlewoods Organisation* v *Harris*). The restriction must also be carefully worded so as to apply only to the side of the business or process that the employee was actually employed in.

Where the danger is customer connection, a non-solicitation covenant alone will almost always suffice. If it is necessary to have a non-competition covenant (perhaps because of the difficulty of proving solicitation or because customers are very likely to follow the employee without his soliciting them) it should be in addition to the non-solicitation covenant and drafted so as to be severable. The covenant should be carefully restricted in area and in the nature of the business so that the employer will not be seen as trying to get too much for his money. Generally, unless there is a very good reason otherwise, the duration should be the same as for the non-solicitation covenant, or even less.

(d) Geographical area

As a general rule, some geographical restriction will be necessary if a non-competition clause is not to be caught by the doctrine. The absence of a geographical restriction will usually lead to its being interpreted as a worldwide restraint, which will in most cases be unreasonably wide. Non-solicitation covenants are restricted by their very nature to areas where the employer had his business and therefore will not normally require a geographical restriction. Similarly, confidential information clauses will not normally be restricted by area because the covenantor and the person to whom he wishes to disclose the information have only to travel outside the area to avoid the express restriction.

If the business is a truly international business, a worldwide restraint may be needed; in any event, if the business extends substantially to a number of countries, those countries should be specified, taking care not to include any country where the business does not really operate. If the client has business in Europe, particular care should be taken to ensure that there is no infringement of Article 85 or 86.

A geographical area which is defined as a radius of a particular number of miles from the place of business has in employment contracts generally been held more acceptable than specifying a particular district, eg "the Greater Manchester area". In a business sale agreement, either definition is probably acceptable. In any event, the area of the vendor's business will already be clear.

The problem for the employer's adviser as opposed to the purchaser's adviser is that the former's business may expand into new areas during the course of the contract. Although an employer (and, for that matter, a vendor) cannot protect an area into which he hopes to expand after termination of the employment, he is entitled nevertheless to protect areas into which he expands during the employment, and the draftsman needs to take this into account so that the clause, although not being too wide, should not be unduly restrictive. This is probably another good reason for using the employer's place or places of business as the centre of the areas to be protected. A clause expressed to prohibit competition "within a radius of five miles of the centre of Oxford" will be of no use to the Oxford employer who subsequently moves his business to Doncaster! One cannot expect the employer who does so to remember to revise his agreements.

The court interprets distances "as the crow flies", and so restricting the covenant to a circle centred on the employer's place or places of business or a well-known local landmark also makes it easier to determine the exact extent of the restriction rather than using the name of a place the boundaries of which are perhaps not so stable or precisely defined.

The actual number of miles involved, if it does not clearly appear to be excessive, is not likely to be regarded as unreasonable of itself, especially if the parties have had an opportunity of discussing it and deciding for themselves that it is a reasonable distance. In determining the area, matters to be taken into consideration might include the strength of customer connection, the incidence of rival firms in the area and the ease with which a customer might change from the client company to a competitor, and whether customers might be prepared to travel and how far they might do so.

(e) Duration

A lifelong restraint is more readily justifiable than a world-wide one if, for example, the protection is required for a trade secret which it is vital should always remain a trade secret or the covenantor's customer connection is so strong or his reputation so wide that any attempt by him to set up in the same line of business is likely to deprive the covenantee of customers. However, where a lifelong restraint is involved, the court will scrutinise the rest of the restriction very carefully to ensure that the covenantor is not prevented from earning a living for the rest of his life. The geographical area and the scope of the business will consequently become more important and must be restricted accordingly.

More often than not, a lifelong restraint will not be justified. The court is likely to regard as lifelong a restraint which is unrestricted as to time. Some duration should usually be attached to the covenant, therefore. A duration which is tantamount to a lifelong restraint is considered as bad as no duration at all. As a rule of thumb, restraints of one to three years have a reasonable chance of succeeding, but restraints of five years and above need stronger justification and will need to be limited in other ways.

If the restraint is reasonable in other ways, the court is unlikely to strike it down on the basis of duration alone. If the parties have agreed a duration which they consider to be reasonable, given the interest to be protected, the area of protection and the likely danger, there should be no problem in using that duration in the clause.

(f) Breaches of confidence

A confidentiality covenant ("not to use or disclose") will provide greater protection than a general non-competition covenant since it need not be limited to trade secrets. Where protection is required for other than obvious trade secrets, however, it may be necessary to define with some precision just what the parties mean by confidential information.

A covenant of this nature is likely to be interpreted with less severity than a non-competition covenant, but the problem for the owner of the information is that he will have to prove actual usage or disclosure – or at least a very strong threat of it – whereas with a non-competition covenant he will need to prove only that the covenantor possesses confidential information amounting to a trade secret and the threat will be assumed. The back-up of a severable non-competition covenant is therefore worth considering.

On the question of defining the information to be caught, some account should be taken of the factors mentioned in Chapters 1, 2 and 3, and some kind of formula might be devised for incorporating these factors. The attention of the owner of the information should, of course, be drawn to these factors so that he does not unwittingly pass on confidential information.

The covenant ought to be restricted to the period during which the information is not in the public domain, and it may be wise to include a provision restraining the covenantor from copying or memorising confidential documents, details of confidential processes etc.

(g) Partnership

A partnership agreement is slightly different from the other kinds of agreement commonly involving restraints. The court has held that it is important to treat partners equally so that a non-solicitation covenant which is restricted to former clients of each particular partner might well be deemed to operate unfairly on a partner with more clients than the others. However, despite dicta in *Bridge* v *Deacons*, one can argue that it is equally unfair to subject a sleeping partner, who has no contact with clients at all, to the same post-dissolution or post-retirement non-solicitation covenant as his active partners.

However, with a partnership agreement it will be easier for the draftsman to tailor the restrictions to the particular partners involved and arrive at restrictions which are both reasonable and fair to all the parties. Perhaps the most important job is to ensure that all the partners understand the restrictions, that they are not "imposed" on anyone and that they are deemed by all the partners to be reasonable, or at least properly negotiated between them.

(h) Reasonableness clauses

A clause which provides that the parties consider the restrictions to be reasonable will probably be void as an attempt to oust the jurisdiction of the courts. It may also be superfluous. Nevertheless, so long as it is clearly seen to be separate and severable, it will do no harm and it may well provide evidence that the parties have negotiated the agreement in good faith and considered the clause to be reasonable at the time the contract was made – something the courts cannot altogether ignore, at least where the parties are on an equal footing.

A clause which enables the court to select whichever version of the contract it considers to be reasonable appears to be effective (at least so long as it can do so by deleting words rather than by re-writing the agreement) and may prompt the court to take a liberal rather than a literal view of the restraints.

3. Examples

The following examples of restraint clauses have been drafted by way of illustration of the drafting points contained in this chapter, and to show different forms of words which may be used. They are not intended to be imported wholesale into any agreement and, if used as a guide to drafting restrictions in an agreement, they should only be used in the context of advice given in this and the preceding chapters, and should be specifically tailored to the client's needs and modified so as to be consistent with the agreement as a whole. Since the question of whether a restraint clause will be held reasonable depends on the particular circumstances of the case, we cannot of course guarantee that any of these restrictions will be upheld in any particular case. (NB: the wording of clauses within the different types of agreement shown is not always consistent because the aim here is to show that different forms of words can be used to obtain the same effect. The wording of clauses within an agreement should as a general rule be consistent.)

I. *Business sale agreement*

Non-Solicitation

1. The Vendor hereby covenants with the Purchaser that from completion hereof, and for the [2] years immediately following the Completion Date, neither he, the Vendor, nor anyone employed by him or acting on his behalf or by or on behalf of a company or firm which he, the Vendor, controls, manages or is interested in, shall approach, canvass, solicit, entice or otherwise contact, directly or indirectly any person who is at the Completion Date, or has been during the past [ ] years a customer of The Business, for the purposes of doing any business the same as or similar to that carried on by The Business at the Completion Date.

Non-Competition

2. The Vendor hereby covenants with the Purchaser that he will not during the [2] years immediately following the Completion Date either directly or indirectly in any capacity whatsoever engage in or be concerned with or interested in any business similar to The Business within a radius of [5] miles from any place where The Business is carried on at the Completion Date.

Confidentiality

3. The Vendor hereby undertakes that he will not for [3] years immediately following the Completion Date either use or disclose to any person in any way whatsoever any confidential information [including trade-secrets, know-how and other confidential information] relating to The Business which shall not have come into the public domain at the Completion Date except where the Vendor is compelled by statute or the common law to disclose such information.

4. The above restrictions are considered by the parties to be reasonable in the circumstances but if such is not the case, the parties agree to abide by such part or parts of the agreement that the court after deletion of the unreasonable part or parts considers to be reasonable in the circumstances.

II. *Director's service contract*

Restrictions During Employment

1. So long as the Director is employed hereunder he shall devote substantially all his time during working hours to carrying out his duties hereunder.

2. The Director agrees that during his employment hereunder he shall not engage or be concerned or interested in any business competing with the business of the Company, PROVIDED THAT the Director shall not be deemed to be concerned or interested in a company if he holds less than [1%] of the issued share capital of that company and neither directly nor indirectly controls nor acts on behalf of that company.

3. The Director agrees that he shall not during his employment hereunder take any steps towards setting up business on his own account (whether in competition with the business of the Company or not) without first informing the Board of Directors of the Company and obtaining their consent to his doing so.

4.(1) The Director undertakes that he will not take the benefit of any contract or business opportunity obtained through or in consequence of his position as Director of the Company (whether or not the Company could have taken the benefit of the said contract or business opportunity or whether or not the Board of Directors of the Company have examined the contract or business opportunity and have rejected it on behalf of the Company) without first obtaining the consent of the Board of Directors of the Company.

(2) If the Director shall obtain such a contract or business opportunity in breach of subclause (1) of this clause, he shall account to the Company for all profits and other benefits received by him in connection with the said contract or business opportunity and shall indemnify the Company in full against any additional loss suffered by the Company as a result of his breach.

(3) This clause shall continue in force notwithstanding termination of this agreement howsoever brought about.

5. The Director undertakes that during his employment hereunder he shall keep confidential all information concerning the business affairs of the Company and any other information which the Board of Directors of the Company shall reasonably regard as confidential (including, but not limited to, trade secrets, know-how, processes, procedures and information concerning employees, suppliers and customers of the Company) and shall not, except properly in the course of his employment hereunder, use or disclose any such

information without the express consent of the Board of Directors of the Company.

Post-Termination Restrictions

6.(1) The Director undertakes that he will not, during the [2] years immediately following termination of his employment hereunder (howsoever terminated) solicit for or on behalf of any competing business any customer or supplier of the Company who was a customer or a supplier of the Company at any time during the period of his employment hereunder.

(2) "solicit" in subclause (1) hereof shall include direct or indirect soliciting, canvassing, enticing away or otherwise contacting for business purposes whether by the Director himself or by a servant or agent acting on his behalf or on behalf of any business in which he is interested.

(3) "competing business" in subclause (1) means any business in which the Director shall be concerned, interested or engaged (on his own account or otherwise) which is similar to the business or any part of the business carried on by the Company.

7.(1) The Director undertakes that for the [2] years immediately following the termination of his employment hereunder, howsoever terminated, he will not deal with any customer or supplier of the Company who was a customer or supplier of the Company at any time during the Director's employment with the Company even though the Director has not solicited the business of the said customer or supplier.

(2) The Director shall be in breach of the covenant contained in subclause (1) of this clause whether he deals with the said customer or supplier directly or indirectly on his own account or in the course of any business in which he is engaged or through any of his servants or agents or any business in which he is concerned or engaged or interested.

(3) The Director shall not be in breach of the covenant contained in subclause (1) unless the dealing prohibited by the clause is in the course of a business competing with the business of the Company.

8. The Director undertakes that he will not during the [2] years immediately following termination hereof engage or be interested in a competing business within a [3] mile radius of any place at which the Company shall be carrying on business now or at the date of termination. "Competing business" has the same meaning as in subclause (3) of clause 6 hereof.

9. The Director undertakes that in the event of this agreement being terminated for any reason whatsoever he shall not at any time within the [12 months] immediately following such determination enter into any contract of service or employment with [A. Rival Ltd.] or with any subsidiary, holding or associate company of [A. Rival Ltd.] or any firm in which [A. Rival Ltd.] shall be a partner, through which a business competing with the business of the Company in [the United Kingdom/Liverpool etc.] may be carried on.

10. The Director undertakes to inform the Company of any unsolicited approach made to him during his employment here-under by or on behalf of [A. Rival Ltd.] or any holding, subsidiary or associate company of [A. Rival Ltd] with a view to his being employed in any capacity which could amount to a breach of Clause 9 hereof.

11. The Director undertakes that he will not following termination of his employment hereunder howsoever terminated (whether law-fully or not) use or disclose any trade secret or confidential infor-mation amounting to a trade secret belonging to the Company.

12.(1) The Director undertakes that he will not within the [2] years immediately following termination of his employment hereunder use or disclose any confidential information of the company.

(2) "Confidential information" in this clause means information:

(a) which has not come into the public domain at the date of termination; and

(b) that the director knows to be confidential or it was imparted to or obtained by the director in such circumstances that he ought to have known it to be confidential; and

(c) that the Board of Directors of the Company reasonably believe would cause material damage to the business of the Company were it to be revealed to or used by any other person, notwithstanding that the information is not a trade secret.

Confidential information is not to be taken to have come into the public domain merely because it is known to other employees of the Company and a limited number of advisers to the Company or other persons dealing with the Company who are or ought to be aware that the Company considers the information to be confidential information.

13. The Director agrees that he will not during his employment or after termination solicit the services of any employee of

of the Company for any other business or make any offer of employment to any such employee.

III. *Contract of employment*

Restrictions During Employment

1. While this agreement continues in force the Employee shall devote substantially the whole of his time during working hours to his duties hereunder.

2. The Employee owes duties of good faith and confidentiality to the Employer. The Employee shall be taken to be in breach of his duty of good faith and/or his duty of confidentiality if, during the continuance of this agreement, he shall (amongst other things):

   (a) engage in any other business or employment whatsoever during working hours;

   (b) engage in any business or employment competing with the business of the Employer during or outside working hours or during bank, statutory or other holidays;

   (c) without the prior written consent of the Employer engage in any business or employment during or outside working hours or during bank, statutory or other holidays in any capacity which may be damaging to the business of the Employer because of the possession by the Employee of confidential information belonging to the Employer or because the Employee has a close connection with or influence over customers of the Employer;

   (d) solicit, canvass or entice the Employer's customers on behalf of any business competing with that of the Employer;

   (e) disclose to any person information belonging to the Employer which the Employee knows to be confidential or which was obtained by or imparted to him in such circumstances that he ought to have known it was confidential information or information that the Employer would not expect him to disclose other than in the course of properly carrying out his duties hereunder;

   (f) copy, photograph, remove or deliberately memorise the contents of any document belonging to the Employer for any purpose other than the proper purposes of his employment hereunder;

   (g) use any information belonging to the Employer which

he knows to be confidential or which was obtained or imparted to him in such circumstances that he ought to have known it was information which the Employer would not expect him to use except in the course of properly carrying out his duties hereunder.

Post-Termination Restrictions

3. If the Employee has had regular direct dealings during the course of h's employment hereunder with any customer of the Employer or has gained influence over any such customer, he shall not during the [2] years immediately following termination of his employment hereunder (terminated by either party and whether lawfully or not) carry on, or be concerned or interested or engage in a similar capacity to the capacity in which he is employed hereunder (or in any other capacity which would make it possible that the said customer or customers would follow him to his new employers) any business similar to or competing with that of the Employer within a [2] mile radius of the Employer's place or any of his places of business.

4. It being recognised by the parties that the Employer shall have imparted to the Employee confidential information to enable him to carry out his duties properly under this agreement, the Employee agrees that he will not [for [   ] years] following termination of his employment hereunder (howsoever terminated), carry on or be engaged or concerned or interested in any business competing with the business of the Employer within [the United Kingdom/Birmingham etc./a radius of [   ] miles from the Employer's place of business etc.].

5. It being accepted by the parties that the Employee [is likely to have access to trade secrets or other confidential information of the Employer in the course of his employment hereunder] [will establish regular/direct/close contact with the Employer's customers], the Employee undertakes not within [2] years following termination of his employment hereunder (howsoever terminated) to enter into employment with [A. Rival Ltd. or any subsidiary, holding or associate company of A. Rival Ltd. which may be carrying on any business competing with the business of the Employer] in a similar capacity to that in which he is employed hereunder.

6. The Employee undertakes that for a period of [2] years following termination of this agreement (whether lawfully terminated or not):

(a)   he will not solicit, canvass or entice for the purposes of any business similar to the Employer's business, any customer of the Employer who was a customer during the period of the Employee's employment with the Employer;

(b) he will not in connection with any business similar to the Employer's business, supply goods [or services] to or otherwise deal with any customer of the Employer who was a customer during the period of the Employee's employment with the Employer.

7. During the period of his employment hereunder and after termination of such employment, the Employee shall not use or disclose:

(a) any confidential information of the Employer obtained in the course of his employment;

(b) any document belonging to the Employer which remains in the Employee's possession after termination of the employment;

and all documents belonging to the Employer in the Employee's possession shall be returned to the Employer and the Employee shall not for his own purposes or those of any person other than the Employer copy, photograph or deliberately memorise the contents of any such document.

8. The Employee undertakes that he will not after termination of his employment hereunder (howsoever terminated) use or disclose any information obtained during the course of his employment which:

(a) is or is tantamount to a trade secret; or

(b) which he knew to be confidential information belonging to the Employer; or

(c) which was imparted to him in such circumstances that he knew or ought to have known that he was expected not to use or disclose it except in the course of his duties hereunder; or

(d) use or disclosure of which the Employer reasonably believed would materially damage his business and the Employee knew or should reasonably have been expected to appreciate that belief.

This clause does not extend to information which is already in the public domain but information is not to be taken to be in the public domain merely because it is known to a restricted number of employees, advisers and others dealing with the Employer.

IV. *Partnership agreement*

Restrictions during the Agreement

1. Each of the Partners undertakes to the other that so long as he remains a Partner in the Firm he will not without the consent of the other Partners (such consent not to be unreasonably withheld) engage or be concerned or interested in any other business similar to or competing with the business of the Partnership, whether or not involving the use of any information or other property of the Partnership.

2. Except with the consent of the other Partners, a Partner shall not during the subsistence of the Partnership, solicit, canvass, or entice any customer of the Partnership Business on behalf of any other business.

3. Each Partner undertakes not to disclose any confidential information of the Partnership (except as required by law) while he is a Partner, such information not being limited to trade secrets but including all other information relating to the Partnership Business which the other Partners would not wish or expect him to disclose except in the proper course of the Partnership Business.

4. Each Partner undertakes not without the consent of the other Partners (such consent not to be unreasonably withheld) to deal with any customer of the Partnership Business in connection with any other business than the Partnership Business.

Post-Retirement Covenants

5. A Retiring Partner (as defined) shall not carry on or be interested, concerned or engaged in any business similar to the Partnership Business within [5] miles of the premises where the Partnership Business is carried on.

6. A Retiring Partner (as defined) shall not carry on business under any name which implies that he is carrying on or is connected with the Partnership Business.

7. A Retiring Partner (as defined) shall not for [2] years following his retirement from the Partnership directly or indirectly, through his servant or agents or those of any business he is engaged, concerned or interested in solicit, canvass, entice or deal with on his own account or on behalf of any other person or business any customer who was a customer of the Partnership Business prior to his retirement.

8. A Retiring Partner (as defined) shall not following his retirement use or disclose (unless required by law to do so) any confidential information relating to the Partnership Business which is tantamount to a trade secret.

9. A Retiring Partner (as defined) shall not following his retirement use or disclose (except under compulsion of law) any information relating to the Partnership or the Partnership Business which:

    (a) he knows to be confidential; or

    (b) he has reason to believe the other Partners would not wish or expect him to use or disclose in view of the potential damage to the Partnership Business caused by such use or disclosure.

10. A Retiring Partner (as defined) shall return to the Continuing Partners (as defined) all documents in his possession relating to the Partnership Business and shall not (unless required by law) without the consent of the Continuing Partners:

    (a) copy, photograph or deliberately memorise the contents of any such documents or cause or permit anyone else to do so; or

    (b) show or cause or permit the documents be shown or reveal their contents to any person who is not a Continuing Partner (as defined); or

    (c) use the said documents or the information contained in them for any purpose other than the purposes of the Partnership Business.

Post-Dissolution Restriction

11. Each Partner undertakes to the other Partners that following dissolution of the Partnership, he will not without the consent of the other Partners carry on a business in any manner or under any name which leads the public to believe that he is carrying on the Partnership Business in succession to the Partnership.

12. Each Partner undertakes to the other Partners that following dissolution he will not without the consent of the other Partners directly or indirectly hold himself out as carrying on the Partnership Business in succession to the Partnership.

13. Each of the Partners agrees that, within the [2] years immediately following dissolution of the Partnership, he will not without the consent of the other Partners (such consent not to be unreasonably withheld) solicit, canvass or deal with any person who was a customer of the Partnership for or on behalf of any business which he

183

carries on, or engages or becomes interested or concerned in.

14. Each of the Partners covenants with the others that he will not during the [5] years immediately following dissolution of the Partnership use or disclose information relating to the Partnership or the Partnership Business which the Partners have agreed is confidential information (whether such information is tantamount to a trade secret or not) except with the consent of the other Partners or under compulsion of law.

15. The Partners believe the restrictions contained in this agreement to be reasonable but should the court hold any part of them to be unreasonable but be prepared to hold that other parts are reasonable the Partners agree to abide by such restrictions or parts of them as the court considers to be reasonable.

Chapter 11

Remedies

1. Breach

In order to obtain any remedy, the plaintiff must at least show that on the face of it there is a valid restriction which the defendant has broken. One problem which arises, particularly with restraint clauses, is whether post-termination restrictions survive the determination of the contract. It seems that where a relationship, eg employer-employee, partnership, principal-agent, is determined properly in accordance with the contract, the contract subsists as regards those clauses which are stated or implied to continue after termination, notwithstanding that the relationship no longer exists. A problem arises, however, when the relationship is improperly determined, ie when one party or the other improperly repudiates the contract.

The general contractual rule is that where a party repudiates or fundamentally breaches the contract, the contract will not automatically come to an end and the innocent party can choose either to accept the breach and bring the contract to an end or refuse to accept it and treat the contract as still in force. The effect of his treating it as still in existence is that the contract remains "alive" so far as both parties are concerned. The innocent party is still bound by his obligations and liabilities under the contract and the other party may therefore not only:

> "complete the contract, if so advised, notwithstanding his previous repudiation of it, but also [to] to take advantage of any supervening circumstance which would justify him in declining to complete it" (Cockburn CJ in *Frost* v *Knight* (1872) 7 Ex 111 at page 112).

Contracts of employment (and indeed other contracts for personal services), however, are difficult to fit within this model. Quite clearly, if an employer wrongfully dismisses an employee, it would be quite wrong to allow him to claim that the post-termination stipulations in the employment contract were still subsisting and to restrain the employee from breaching them, and the court will not do so: *General Billposting Co Ltd* v *Atkinson* (1909). In that case, the defendant was the manager of a billposting company in Newcastle. His contract of employment provided that he should hold office subject to termination at twelve months' notice by either party. It contained a post-termination restraint clause to the effect that he should not, while in the employment of the company or within two years afterwards, carry on a similar business within a specific radius of Newcastle without the company's permission. The defendant was dismissed without notice and successfully sued the company for wrongful dismissal. He then set up a bill posting business within the restricted area. The plaintiff company who had taken over his former employers sued for an injunction and for damages for breach of contract. The House of Lords held that the defendant was no longer bound by the restrictions in his contract as a result of the employer's repudiation.

In a similar vein, it was seen in Chapter 4 how the dissolution of a partnership meant that an employee of the partnership was no longer bound by the covenants in restraint of trade in his contract of employment (*Briggs* v *Oates*).

However, there is some doubt as to whether the employee, as the innocent party, has the right to claim that the contract is still alive, for example because he wishes to claim post-termination commission. There is conflicting authority. On the one hand there are dicta to suggest that, however ready and willing to serve the dismissed employee may be, he has no alternative but to treat the contract as discharged (per Salmon LJ in *Denmark Productions Ltd* v *Boscobel Productions Ltd* (1968)), because of the rule (referred to below) that the court will not order specific performance of a contract for personal services against the employer, and the principle of mutuality requires that where an order would not be granted at the suit of one party, it will not be granted on behalf of the other. However, there are dicta the other way in *Decro-Wall International SA* v *Practitioners in Marketing Ltd* (1971) and in *Gunton* v *Richmond-upon-Thames London Borough Council* (1980) where the majority of the Court of Appeal thought that a dismissal following the carrying out of disciplinary procedures which were technically irregular was ineffective to terminate the employee's employment, although, as it happened, it did not make much difference to that particular case.

Although the employer may wish to keep the contract alive when the employee has breached post-termination restrictions, the employee may be the party who has committed the repudiatory breach. If the court is prepared to take the employee's part and follow the line that contracts of employment are an exception to the general rule, it will not enforce post-termination restrictions in the contract: to hold that contracts of employment are exactly the same as other kinds of contract and subject to the "acceptance of repudiation" rule will mean that the restrictions (if reasonable) will be upheld. This was the situation in *Thomas Marshall (Exports) Ltd* v *Guinle* (1979) where the employee had committed breaches of his duties of good faith to his employer by setting up his own competing business and soliciting his employer's customers and suppliers. Not without admitting the difficulties, Sir Robert Megarry VC, after carefully reviewing all the authorities, considered *inter alia* that for him to hold that contracts of employment were a special case would mean that cases where the courts had enforced a negative restriction, notwithstanding that it might be tantamount to ordering specific performance of a contract for personal services (see below), had been wrongly decided. It is clear, however, that he was influenced in part by the argument that the court should not permit a wrongdoer to profit from his wrongdoing.

The difficulty is to establish a general rule; unfortunately, whether a party to a contract for personal services can claim that the contract subsists or not, seems to depend on the circumstances and what remedy is being claimed.

2. Injunctions

Where the covenantee discovers that the covenantor has broken, or intends to break, his restrictive covenant, the most likely remedy that he will seek will be an injunction.

Injunctions are granted only if the court believes that monetary compensation would be an inadequate remedy. The type of injunction which will usually be sought is prohibitory – to prevent the covenantor from breaking his covenant. An injunction will not be granted for a breach which the covenantor has already committed and which he cannot or will not repeat. And an injunction will not be granted if the defendant gives an undertaking which has the equivalent effect of granting an injunction.

As an injunction is an equitable remedy, the usual equitable principles apply. The court has a discretion to refuse the injunction and to award damages instead. The court will award damages if they would be an adequate remedy or if the injury caused to the plaintiff is slight or if damages would be a more suitable remedy than an injunction. The plaintiff must "come with clean hands". That is to say, he must not have misled the defendant or the court and must not have failed to perform his part of the contract. As we observed from *General Billposting Co Ltd* v *Atkinson* (see page 186), wrongful dismissal will be a ground for refusing an injunction to an employer. Delay (laches) will be a bar, and the plaintiff must seek the court's assistance as promptly as possible. Moreover, the plaintiff will be barred from his action if he has affirmed or acquiesced in the breach.

In considering whether to grant an injunction to uphold a restrictive covenant given by an employee, partner or agent of the plaintiff, the court is faced with a dilemma due to the potential conflict between two principles. The first principle is that the court will always grant an injunction to restrain a breach of a negative covenant. This principle is contained in dicta of Lord Cairns LC in *Doherty* v *Allman* (1878):

> "If parties, for valuable consideration, with their eyes open, contract that a particular thing shall not be done, all that a Court of Equity has to do is to say, by way of injunction, that which the parties have already said by way of covenant, that the thing shall not be done."

In other words the court is not, by granting an injunction, doing any more than specifically enforcing the contract which the parties have made, and thus the usual principles applicable to injunctions – for example whether the plaintiff has suffered any injury or whether an injunction should, on the balance of convenience, be granted in that particular case – do not apply.

The conflicting principle, however, is that the court will not grant an injunction which would be tantamount to granting an injunction for the specific performance of a contract for personal services. This latter is something the court will not do in any circumstances, and it is irrelevant whether the agreement is an employer-employee agreement or another kind of agreement.

In *Thomas Marshall (Exports) Ltd* v *Guinle*, where the court was faced with that particular problem, Sir Robert Megarry VC said:

"If without just cause a servant who has contracted to serve for a term of years refuses to do so, it is easy to see that the court is powerless to make him do what he has contracted to do: neither by decreeing specific performance nor by granting an injunction ..."

The dilemma for the court lies in the fact that if it were to grant a decree of specific performance or order performance by injunction, and should the employee refuse to comply, the court would have no alternative but to commit him to prison which, since it would deprive the employer of his services anyway, would have the opposite effect to what the employer was asking the court to do.

In *Ehrman* v *Bartholomew* (1898) a wine merchants' traveller was employed under a ten-year service contract which provided that he was to devote the whole of his time during usual business hours to the business of the firm and not engage in any other business or transact any business with or for any other person. After about a year, the defendant left the firm and joined another firm of wine merchants. The court refused to restrain him from doing so.

This approach was followed in a more recent case (*Page One Records Ltd* v *Britton* (1967)) where the defendants, a group of pop musicians, appointed the plaintiffs as their managers for five years under a world-wide agreement. The agreement provided that the plaintiffs would use their best endeavours to advance the defendants' careers and that the defendants would not engage any other person to act as their manager or agent. In 1967 the defendants, who had become successful through the plaintiffs' efforts, sought to repudiate the agreement. The plaintiffs, pending trial of a breach of contract action, sought an interlocutory injunction restraining the defendants engaging anyone else as their manager. The injunction was refused on the ground that it would be tantamount to enforcing a contract for personal services.

However, where the restriction is not so wide as to prevent the defendant from engaging in any business, ie earning his living by any means at all, the courts have resolved their dilemma by granting an injunction on the ground that the defendant can always do something else. In *Lumley* v *Wagner* (1852) the defendant was a singer who agreed with the plaintiff to sing at his theatre in London for a period of three months and not to sing for anyone else during that time. She breached her agreement by singing for someone else for a larger amount, but the court was able to grant an injunction concerning the negative part (not to sing for anyone else) while refusing to grant specific performance of the positive part (singing for the plaintiff). The reasoning behind this was that the threat of punishment might induce the lady to perform but would not necessarily compel a good performance and the court could not judge between a bad performance which was naturally bad and one which was deliberately bad. Equally, the court will not order specific performance of an agreement requiring constant supervision, and a contract of employment might also fall within that class of contracts.

Thus, where the negative covenant is attached to or ancillary to a positive covenant, the court finds itself able to give a remedy in respect of the negative part. In the well-known case of *Warner Bros Pictures Inc* v *Nelson* (1937), the court granted an injunction restraining the actress, Bette Davis, from breaching a covenant in a contract for exclusive services which restrained her from rendering services in any motion picure or stage production for anyone save the film company, on the ground that it did not prevent her earning a living in any other capacity, and albeit that the practical effect was to force her to perform her contract for personal services with the film company as surely as if the court had granted an order for specific performance. (However the recent exclusive services cases referred to in earlier chapters, though they clearly have points of distinction, may have cast doubt upon this principle.)

The courts therefore draw a dubious distinction between the two types of case; this may indicate that they dislike the line of authority begun in *Lumley* v *Wagner* and are prepared to adopt a device which does not force them to follow it. Perhaps it was this dislike of the principle which forced the House of Lords to take the line they did in *Schroeder Music Publishing Co* v *Macaulay* and *Clifford Davies Management Ltd* v *WEA Records Ltd*.

Interlocutory injunctions

The purpose of an interlocutory injunction is to preserve the status quo pending a proper trial of the proceedings. If, for example, an ex-employer discovers that his former employee is, contrary to his contract of employment, soliciting the employer's customers for his own business, the employer could be caused a great deal of damage, probably irreparable, in the months that it takes the action to come to full trial. The court may therefore, in proper circumstances, be prepared in the meantime to restrain the former employee by interlocutory injuncticn.

The modern principles for the hearing of proceedings for an

interlocutory injunction were set out by the House of Lords in *American Cyanamid Co* v *Ethicon Ltd* (1975), in particular in the judgment of Lord Diplock ([1975] AC 396 at page 407). The first principles are as follows:

(i) the court should not at the interlocutory stage try to make a proper assessment of the facts of the case;

(ii) nor should it hear and decide detailed argument on questions of law;

(iii) if the available material fails to show that the plaintiff has any real prospect of succeeding in a claim for a permanent injunction, the court will not grant an interlocutory injunction;

(iv) if (iii) is not in fact the case, the court should then go on to consider whether, on the balance of convenience, an interlocutory injunction should be granted, or whether it should be refused.

In other words, the *American Cyanamid* principle, which is aimed at speeding up interlocutory hearings, requires that the plaintiff merely must show that he has some real prospect of succeeding in a claim for a permanent injunction. The hearing is not a trial of the issues as it so often was before 1975. However, this is not always the case in the kind of action with which we are here concerned. The issues are often so vital and immediate that what is decided at the interlocutory stage will decide the action. The plaintiff who has already suffered substantial damage may suffer irreparably if the defendant is not restrained and the defendant may find his own business substantially impaired or himself out of a job if he is restrained in the interlocutory proceedings, with what is decided later being of far less importance. In a number of cases, therefore, the court will be prepared to hear the whole story and, in effect, try the issues.

If the *American Cyanamid* approach is taken, there is a second stage: the court must consider whether damages would be an adequate remedy if the plaintiff were to succeed on a full trial of the action. It is of course a fundamental principle that an injunction cannot be granted where damages would be an adequate remedy, and it is the court's task at this stage to look at the period between the interlocutory application and the trial and consider whether, if the plaintiff were to win his case, he would be adequately compensated for the continuing damage which the defendant's conduct inflicted upon him during that period. If that is the case, an interlocutory injunction will not be granted.

The same test should then be applied to the defendant. In the kind of case we are considering, of course, the defendant could suffer at least as much damage as the plaintiff: if, for example, he has set up his own business, being restrained for several weeks or even months from being able to continue it may cause irreparable damage to that business and will also cause him personal financial difficulties.

If it appears that damages would not be an appropriate remedy for either party, the court must then go on to consider the balance of convenience. In other words it must perform a weighing-up exercise between the relative situations of the plaintiff and the defendant to determine whether it would be more "inconvenient" to the plaintiff not to grant the injunction pending trial than it would be to the defendant if it were granted. It can be seen why this approach is not appropriate where the damage to either party would be considerable.

Similar bars to the granting of an interlocutory injunction apply as with a permanent injunction; conditions may be imposed, the most usual being that the plaintiff gives an undertaking in damages and, possibly, pays something into court.

Procedure is by way of a hearing in open court in the Chancery Division or by judge in chambers in the Queen's Bench Division. Two clear days' notice should be issued with the writ or summons; but if the matter is one of great urgency, or if pressure of business in the courts prevents a prompt hearing of an opposed application, it may be heard *ex parte* (in the absence of the other party).

Acting in breach of an injunction is considered a very serious matter and may result in fines, sequestration or committal to prison.

3. Damages

The question of whether to go for an injunction or for damages will depend on whether the plaintiff has suffered, or is likely to suffer, injury to his business. Although an injunction is the usual remedy to be sought because it will protect the plaintiff both now and for the future, there is always the possibility that the defendant will have already acted in such a way as to damage the plaintiff's interests before the action. In this case, an injunction will not restore to the plaintiff what he has lost and he will wish to seek compensation by way of damages.

The court itself may decide that the plaintiff's remedy should be in damages either because damages will afford an adequate remedy – and the court will not, or course, grant an injunction in this case – or because the court is unwilling to grant an injunction for another reason, for example because it would be tantamount to ordering specific performance of a contract for personal services, or because the injury to the plaintiff is so slight that an injunction is inappropriate. An injunction will not be granted to remedy a mere inconvenience. The court will not, on the other hand, allow a wrong to continue simply because the wrongdoer is willing and able to pay for the injury he causes (see *Kelsen* v *Imperial Tobacco Co (of Great Britain and Ireland) Ltd* (1957)).

In *Shelfer* v *City of London Electric Lighting Co* (1895), a case of nuisance, it was said that a "good working rule" is to refuse an injunction and only award damages where there is a small injury which is capable of being estimated in money and adequately compensated by a small sum and the grant of an injunction would be oppressive. This "working rule", however, is merely a rule of guidance and has often been departed from in later cases. The court must consider all the circumstances of the case, including the conduct of the defendant, the plaintiff's intentions and any benefit which may have accrued to the plaintiff from the defendant's breach. A finding that damages are an adequate remedy is, as mentioned above, a bar to the granting of an interlocutory injunction.

Where damages are awarded as a substitute for an injunction, they must cover all the things that the injunction would have covered so that the plaintiff will be compensated for any injury he might suffer in the future.

(a) Unliquidated damages

In most cases where damages are awarded, and especially where they are awarded in substitution for an injunction, they will be unliquidated damages which it is the court's task to assess. The fact that damages, at least so far as the future is concerned, are difficult to assess will be no bar to the plaintiff's claim.

The assessment of unliquidated damages will follow the usual rules as set out in *Hadley* v *Baxendale* (1854), ie the plaintiff will be compensated for:

(i) damages which may fairly and reasonably be considered as arising naturally from the breach, ie according to the usual course of things; and

(ii) damages which may reasonably be supposed to have been in the contemplation of both parties at the time they made the contract as the probable result of the breach.

Although attempts have been made to re-formulate the rule in succeeding cases, the intention behind the rule appears to be reasonably clear.

Damages under the first head will be awarded for those consequences which flow so naturally from the breach that any reasonable person would expect them. An example in the sphere with which we are dealing is that if a defendant employee had built up a good following among his employer's customers and then left his employer to set up his own business in the neighbourhood, the natural consequence is that some at least of his employer's clientele would follow him. The consequential damage is the resultant loss of profit to the employer, for which he would be compensated.

The second head is more difficult and appears from the facts of *Hadley* v *Baxendale* to require some special circumstances known to the parties over and above what is obvious to everyone. In *Victoria Laundry (Windsor) Ltd* v *Newman Industries Coulson & Co Ltd* (1949) the plaintiffs were launderers and dyers. They ordered a larger boiler from the defendant engineering company so that they could carry out some extremely lucrative dyeing contracts, telling them that they were most anxious to use the boiler in the shortest possible time. There was a long delay in delivery and the plaintiffs were allowed to claim loss of profit through their inability to extend their business during the period, although not the full amount of the loss of the "highly lucrative" dyeing contracts the prospect of which was not disclosed to the defendants. The special circumstances in this case were that the defendants, as well as the plaintiffs, could reasonably be expected to suppose that some loss of profit would result from the plaintiffs' inability to extend their business.

Injury under this heading might therefore result to the plaintiff because the defendant is possessed of a particular piece of confidential information which, if disclosed to a rival, may place the rival in a substantially better position to compete with the plaintiff. Matters within the reasonable contemplation of the parties are assessed as at the date of the contract.

The duty to mitigate applies to this type of damage as to others. It is not, however, clear what steps the plaintiff might take by way of mitigation in this case. If a defendant employee or vendor of a business deliberately woos away the plaintiff's customers, is it sufficient for the plaintiff to sit back and claim damages or should he take some steps to woo them back? There is little that a plaintiff can do where his employee is in possession of confidential information, but what about preventing him from joining a rival company? In *Littlewoods Organisation v Harris* (where an injunction was sought) there was no suggestion that the plaintiff should have engaged in an "auction" with a rival company for the former employee's services, although the plaintiff might well have been able to do so. Some attempts, however, had been made to keep the defendant in the plaintiff's employment. What if the plaintiff simply does nothing and lets his employee go to work for a rival? The answer is probably that, even if damages rather than an injunction are claimed, this will not affect the plaintiff's claim. The rule is that mitigation is not required until a breach has been accepted (*White and Carter (Councils) Ltd v McGregor* (1961)) and so in most cases it will be too late for the plaintiff to do anything.

(b) Liquidated damages

The court may be faced with a claim for damages because the parties have stipulated in the contract a sum payable by the defendant to the plaintiff on breach. The problem is that liquidated damages must be distinguished from penalty clauses. Liquidated damages are a genuine pre-estimate of the loss which the plaintiff can recover without having to prove actual damage. A penalty, however, is a threat or security that the contract will be performed. Very often, particularly in cases such as those we are concerned with here, it will be extremely difficult to distinguish between the two.

The importance of the distinction is this: where the amount stipulated in the contract is less than the amount of the actual damage suffered by the plaintiff, the plaintiff is restricted in his claim to the actual amount of his loss if the stipulation is a penalty clause − but if the clause is for liquidated damages, he can recover the whole amount stated in the contract, although he has made a profit. Where, on the other hand, the amount stipulated in the contract is more than the actual damage suffered, if the stipulation is a penalty clause, the plaintiff can probably forgo it and sue under breach of contract for compensation for his actual loss (although there appears to be some doubt about this and he will not be able to do so if the contract clearly shows that recovery of the stipulated amount is his only right) − but if it is a liquidated damages clause, he is restricted to the amount stipulated, although he has made a loss.

The question is therefore likely to be a very important one. The intention is to be discovered from an examination of the contract

as a whole — the words used by the parties to describe the payment
are not conclusive. The court must look to the substance rather
than the form. It is a question of construction to be decided upon
the terms and circumstances of each contract as at the time the
contract was made, not at the time of breach. In *Dunlop Pneumatic
Tyre Co Ltd* v *New Garage and Motor Co Ltd* (1915) the guidelines
which the judges were accustomed to use were summarised by Lord
Dunedin. The following, in order of importance, are relevant to a
restrictive clause:

(i)   the stipulated amount will be a penalty if extravagant and
unconscionable in comparison with the greatest loss that
could possibly be the consequence of the breach;

(ii)   the stipulated amount will be liquidated damages if it is
to be paid on the occurrence of a single event;

(iii)   if several events are stipulated, the happening of one,
more or all of which may require payment of a single
lump sum, and some of the events are serious and others
trifling, there is a presumption that the stipulated amount
is a penalty;

(iv)   if it is virtually impossible to prove the exact loss consequential on the events stipulated, then the amount, if
reasonable, is more likely to be liquidated damages.

Although equity deplores a penalty, the courts will take great care
in deciding into which category the clause falls; the courts will not
be too quick to dismiss it as a penalty clause. A clause which
tries to assess the damage in advance of breaching the contract
is a useful tool for both plaintiff and defendant because it makes
the consequences of the breach certain and is an attempt to avoid
expensive litigation on the question of actual loss. The inclusion
of a penalty clause is, however, no bar to the granting of an
injunction. A liquidated damages clause is therefore something
the parties might be inclined to consider. However, making a
pre-estimate of the damage which will be caused to the plaintiff's
business will, in most cases, be even more difficult at the time of
the contract than after breach has occurred.

(c) Damages in addition to an injunction

Lord Cairns' Act 1858 gave the Chancery Court the power to
award damages to the injured party either in addition to or
in substitution for an injunction or specific performance, and
the Judicature Act 1873 provided that the High Court and the
Court of Appeal should grant "all such remedies whatsoever as

the parties may appear to be entitled to in respect of any legal or equitable claim". There is therefore no doubt as to the power of the courts to award damages in addition to an injunction. However, for them to do so is a fairly rare occurrence and the plaintiff must show special reasons why an injunction or damages alone would not remedy his injuries. Such a situation might perhaps occur where the plaintiff has already suffered substantial damage before the matter has come to trial, and damages are required to compensate him for what has already happened as well as an injunction to secure him against the defendant's wrongdoing for the future.

(d) Statutory time limits

The limitation periods under the Limitation Act 1980 are six years for an action under a simple contract and twelve years for an action on a contract under seal. Time will begin to run against the plaintiff from the date when the defendant first breaches the contract, not when the plaintiff discovers the breach. Time will run from the later date (under s 32) only if (a) the action is based upon the fraud of the defendant; or (b) any fact relevant to the plaintiff's right of action has been deliberately concealed from him by the defendant; or (c) the action is for relief from the consequences of a mistake. If the plaintiff was an infant or of unsound mind when the cause of action accrued, there will be an extension of time to cover the relevant period when he was suffering from the disability.

4. Declarations

Either party may ask the court for a declaration of his rights in the matter in question. This is a useful half-way house whereby the defendant can obtain the court's ruling as to whether a contractual restriction to which he is subject is binding, without running the risk of an injunction or damages. Equally, the plaintiff may seek the court's ruling in order to ascertain whether he is likely to succeed in an action, thus forming the basis of negotiations for compensation.

The remedy – the power to award which is given to the Supreme Court by the Judicature Acts 1873–75, regardless of whether or not consequential relief may be obtained – is discretionary but is not a form of equitable relief (despite dicta of Denning LJ in *Barnard* v *National Dock Labour Board* (1953)). The remedy is not therefore subject to equitable principles such as the rule that "he who seeks equity must do equity" (*Chapman* v *Michaelson* (1909)), and presumably is not subject to the equitable bars.

5. Assignment of rights and remedies

The benefit of negative restrictions in a contract (if any) may be assigned as a chose in action in the same way as any other contractual benefit, and the rights and remedies of the covenantee on breach by the covenantor will accrue to the assignee. In other words, the covenantee may assign the whole contract in the usual way, ie in law by an absolute assignment in writing, or in equity where there is a clear intention to assign, and the assignee will take the benefit of any negative restrictions.

However, the covenantor cannot assign any positive covenant for personal services. Equally, if the covenant is expressed so as to be personal to the covenantee it will not be assignable (*Davies* v *Davies* (1887); *Berlitz School of Languages Ltd* v *Duchêne* (1903)). It is therefore necessary to read the wording of the covenant carefully if an assignment is contemplated. If it cannot be assigned, the only way in which the assignee of the agreement could enforce it would be by novation and fresh consideration might be required.

Generally speaking, however, the covenants are assignable and the purchaser of the goodwill of a business is able to enforce earlier covenants taken by his vendor for the protection of the goodwill (*Elves* v *Crofts* (1850)), and on a take-over of a company the new owner is able to enforce the covenants against former employees (*Home Counties Dairies Ltd* v *Skilton*).

In conclusion, therefore, the *covenantee*, his successors and assignees, will have available to them the following remedies in the English courts:

- Damages, where these will adequately compensate him

  - damages may be awarded for breach of a covenant in restraint and possibly for an infringement of Article 85 or 86;
  - damages may be awarded to compensate him for all the loss he has sustained from the date of the breach or infringement up to the date of the trial;
  - he may obtain an unliquidated award or he may be entitled to liquidated damages specified in the contract.

- A permanent injunction

- an injunction will be awarded only where damages will not adequately compensate the covenantee;
- an injunction will not be awarded where there are any bars such as long delay, affirmation etc;
- an injunction will not be awarded if it would have the effect of forcing the other party to perform a contract for personal services.

- An interlocutory injunction

  - will be awarded only in the circumstances described above for the award of a permanent injunction;
  - will be awarded only if the balance of convenience favours the covenantee;
  - will often be the deciding factor in the case.

- A declaration of rights

  - is not subject to equitable principles;
  - may be made when the covenantor is no longer in breach (eg because the covenant has expired);
  - may found a claim for damages or assist the parties in negotiating compensation.

The *covenantor* may claim:

- A declaration of rights

  - to enable him to establish that he may take on a particular job;
  - to found a claim for damages where the covenantor has prevented him from taking on particular employment;
  - to establish the limits of what he is prevented from doing.

A declaration may be founded on the basis that:

- the clause is too wide; or
- the agreement has terminated in such a way that post-termination restrictions are no longer binding; or
- a purported assignee or other successor is not entitled to enforce the covenant.

A full range of remedies is therefore provided for both parties.

Index